LEAN SIX SIGMA
GREEN BELT
HANDBOOK

To the magic of my life...my husband...

Text Copyright © 2017 Shweta Ravi

All Rights Reserved

Preface

This book is designed for the individuals interested in learning the concept of six sigma. The six sigma certification exam has different levels known as belts. Green Belt is responsible for executing and completing the project, finalize other team members for the project, define scope and goal with the champion, work in close collaboration with Black Belt to conduct required statistical analysis, ensure proposed solutions implemented, and track sustenance of improvement in control phase. The green belt can either be a process owner or a team member who has visibility on the challenges faced on a daily basis.

This book will be a perfect guide if you want to understand and implement six sigma methodology for problem-solving. I have tried to keep the explanation short and simple so that it's easier to understand. The book doesn't get into details of how to do the statistical analysis as that's in the purview of black belt. But all relevant statistical topics are covered and explained to meet the requirement of green belt certification.

I hope you find this content helpful. Please log on to my blog *shwetaravi.com* to leave feedback and download process excellence templates for free.

Contents

Preface .... *vi*

Part 1: Lean Six Sigma *1*

Introduction Six Sigma 2
    History 2
    What is Six Sigma? 2

Lean Overview 8
    Ford Motors 8
    Toyota Production Systems 9

Lean Six Sigma 17
    DMAIC 17

Part 2: Define *22*

Project identification 23
    Prioritization and Selection of Improvement Opportunity 23
    Balance Scorecard 23

Critical to Quality 25
    Introduction to CTQ 25
    Key Performance Indicator 25
    Voice of Customer 33
    Kano Model 35

Project Charter 37

Project Goal 38
SIPOC 39
Team Charter 41
    ARMI Model 42

Part 3: Measure *44*

Data Types 45
Basic Statistics 47
    Measure of central tendency 47
    Quartile 48
    Kurtosis 49
    Skewness 49
    Measure of dispersion 50
Data Collection Planning 53
Sampling 55
    Sample Type 55
Measurement System Analysis 58
    Measurement System Characteristics 58
    Gage Linearity and Bias 62
    Gage Reproducibility and Repeatability (GR&R) 64
    .Attribute Agreement Analysis 67
Process Capability 71
    C_p 71
    C_{pk} 72
Sigma Level 73
    Sigma Level for Attribute data 74
    Sigma Level for Continuous data 75

Process Variation 76
   Common and Special Variation 76
   Histogram 76
   Dot Plot 77
   Box Plot 78
   Run Chart 80
   Probability Distribution 81

Part 4: Analyze 85

Process Mapping – VA NVA Analysis 86

Failure Mode Effect Analysis (FMEA) 91

Cause Effect diagram 94

Gemba Walk 95

Correlation 96

Regression 98
   Simple Linear Regression 98
   Multilinear regression 100

Hypothesis Testing 103
   Type I & Type II Error 104
   Hypothesis Test Roadmap 106
   Parametric Hypothesis Test (continuous normal data) 108
   Non-Parametric Test (Continuous Non-normal data) 118
   Binomial Hypothesis Test 121

Part 5: Improve 123

Idea Generation 124
   Benchmarking 124
   Brainstorming 125

Lean Tools 127
    5S 127
    Visual Andon 130
    Poka-Yoke 130

Selection and Prioritization of Solution 132
    Pugh Matrix 132
    Multi-voting 134

Introduction to Design of Experiment 135

Validation of Improvement 139

Part 6: Control *140*

Process Control Plan 141

Statistical Process Control 143
    Control chart roadmap 143
    Control Limits 143

Institutionalize Solution 146

Project Closure 147

Part 1: Lean Six Sigma

Introduction Six Sigma

History

Six Sigma is a data-driven methodology first introduced in the 1970s. Dr. Mikel Harry, the senior staff at Motorola, was the first one to try statistical problem-solving. Later on Bill Smith, an engineer at Motorola designed six-step methodology to reduce variation and considered as the Father of Six Sigma.

In 1995, Jack Welch made Six Sigma the center of business strategy at General Electrical. Employees at GE had to undertake 13 days of six sigma training and complete one project by the end of 1998. Jack Welch achieved his goal of becoming a Six Sigma company by the end of 2000. During this period, GE reported saving of approximately $12 billion. Since then, Six Sigma is adopted by various companies to improve their top and the bottom line like Samsung, Amazon, Dell to name a few.

What is Six Sigma?

'Sigma (σ)' is a Greek alphabet which means standard deviation. 'Six Sigma' literally means *six* standard deviation.

Let's first try to understand standard deviation and then we will get to the significance of 'six standard deviations.'

Standard deviation

The standard deviation represents the variation of data points from the mean.

For example, if the average marks scored by a class is 73 out of 100 for a particular subject. This doesn't mean that all students have got 73 marks, there will be variation in scores. Let's assume; we just have five students in the class, who have got 68, 52, 85, 90, 70 marks in the exam.

$$Average\ marks = Mean = \frac{68 + 52 + 85 + 90 + 70}{5} = 73$$

The variation of scores from the average is -5, -21, 12, 17, -3, which will sum up to zero. Hence we can't directly calculate the average of variations. The standard deviation is calculated using the square of the variations.

$$Std.\ Deviation\ for\ population = \sqrt{\frac{(Xi - \overline{X})^2}{n}}$$

In this scenario, it's easy to consider whole population i.e. marks of all the students.

But let's say for calculating per capita income for a country, it's difficult to collect data for all citizens. Hence, you will have to take the sample.

$$Std\ Deviation\ for\ sample = \sqrt{\frac{(Xi - \bar{X})^2}{n-1}}$$

Divide the sum of the square of variations by (n-1) for calculating the standard deviation for sample data. 'n' or 'n-1' won't make much difference if the sample size is big enough

The significance of six standard deviations

Let's assume '50' is the passing marks of the student. In six sigma language, '50' is the lower specification limit, anything below which is not acceptable.

Figure 1 shows the histogram of student's marks. The mean for considered data is 73, and the standard deviation is 16.46. You can fit 1.4 ([73-50]/16.46) standard deviation between mean and lower specification limit. Hence this process is performing at 1.4 sigma level.

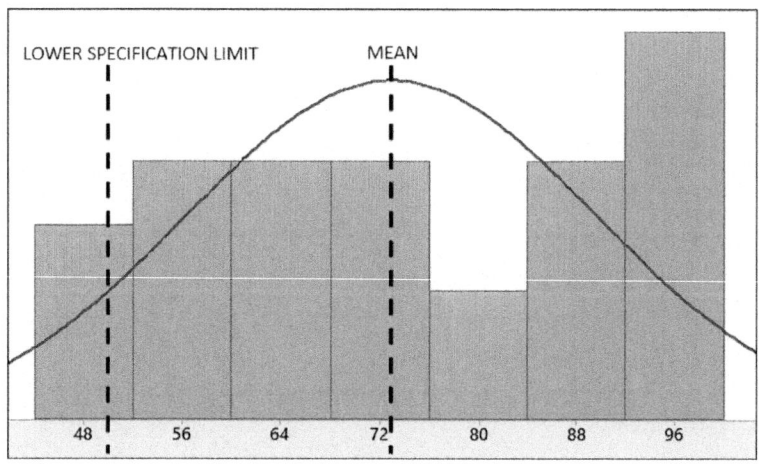

<u>Figure 1: Student's marks</u>

Different companies, also various processes within a company will have various performance measure criteria. Sigma level is the standard criteria used to compare the process performance. You can convert any measurement parameter to sigma level.

But why six sigma?

In statistics, you can fit 68.27% of data within +/- 1 standard deviation of the mean. This means 68.27% students will get marks between 57 (73-16.46) and 90 (73-16.46). Similarly, 95.46% can fit within +/- 2 standard deviations, and 99.73% are within +/- 3 standard deviations.

In simple language, if the process is performing at 3 Sigma level i.e. three standard deviations can fit between mean and specification limit, then 99.73% data points will meet the process specification.

Moreover, if the process is six sigma, 99.9997% data will meet the process specification, or you will make only 3.4 defects per million opportunities. Naturally, the process can achieve more than six sigma. However, for most of the industries, six sigma level is considered as an excellent achievement except for the industries like health care or aviation.

Figure 2 shows the defect per million opportunities achieved at each sigma level. For now, don't worry about short-term sigma level, we will discuss this in detail in the coming chapters.

Short term sigma level (Zst)	DPMO
6	3.4
5.5	31.7
5	233
4.5	1350
4	6210
3.5	22750
3	66811
2.5	158687
2	308770
1.5	501350
1	697672

Figure 2: Sigma Level

Lean Overview

Ford Motors

Lean philosophy means achieving more by using fewer resources. An efficient way of working with limited wastage in the system. The Ford assembly line system used to develop Model T allowed Ford to sell his cars at a price lower than his competitors due to the efficiency of the system.

In early 1910, Henry Fort developed a continuous manufacturing unit to build the all-time famous Model T. The Model T recognized as the first affordable class, hence opening a big market of middle-class Americans. Model T sales reached the highest of all time which made Henry the richest man of that time. Many industries tried to copy the continuous production philosophy with least success. Model T was available in only one color, black. Henry Ford wrote in his autobiography that the instruction to the management was "Any customer can have a car painted any color that he wants so long as it is black." As other companies started to offer other options to the competitive market, Model T lost his dominance and overtaken by General Motors car.

Toyota Production Systems

The American industry progression caught Japanese companies' attention. Kiichiro Toyoda, founder of Toyota Motor Corporation and Taiichi Ohno, an Industrial engineer at Toyota decided to look into Henry Ford's flow production model. Though flow production model was very successful, it failed to generate the variety of products.

Taiichi Ohno incorporated Ford's strategy and other quality methods inspired by Ishikawa, Deming, and Juran. Kiichiro Toyoda's belief that "the ideal conditions for making things are created when machines, facilities, and people work together to add value without generating any waste" led him to remove waste between the operations. The result was the Just-in-Time method. Later Eiji Toyoda with the help of Taiichi Ohno realized 'Toyota Production System' which is the foundation of Lean methodology. Ohno is considered as the Father of Toyota Production System.

Toyota published the first official version of Toyota Production system (TPS) in 1990. As per most recent version, TPS has three desired outcomes:

- To provide the customer with the highest quality vehicles, at lowest possible cost, promptly with the shortest possible lead times.

- To give members with work satisfaction, job security and fair treatment.
- It gives the company flexibility to respond to the market, achieve profit through cost reduction activities and long-term prosperity.

TPS focus on eliminating Waste (Muda), Unevenness (Mura) and Overburden (Muri) from the system. Figure 3 pictorially represent all key concepts of Toyota Production System.

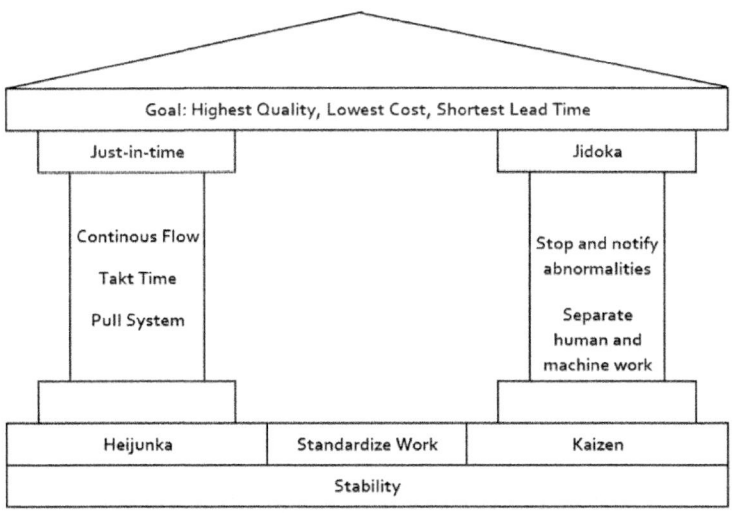

Figure 3: Toyota Production System

Now, let's looks at the components of Toyota Production Model.

Just-in-time

Toyota engineers first introduced and used the word 'Just-in-time,' which means producing only the required amount at the right time. The natural law of demand and supply drives just-in-time philosophy. Customer demand will define how many vehicles to build, the number of the vehicles will drive the number of parts or materials ordered, and the chain goes on. Hence, ensures only desired number of vehicles produced, to achieve less inventory and better efficiency.

Takt time

Takt time gives the linkage between customer demand and production. Takt time is the rate at which order should be produced to meet customer demand with available resources.

For example, if a plant is operating for 8 hours per day and the demand is 80 vehicles, the takt time is 0.1 hours (8/80) i.e. one car needs to produce every 30 minutes. Another example of service industries could be, ten employees are working in an office for 8 hours per day. The available production hours are 80 per day and if 80 is the demand, then takt time is 1 hour (80/80).

Continuous Flow

Continuous flow or One-piece flow is producing one item at a time. Once an item is in production, it should continuously move through the production line until delivered to the client. Each step should only produce the quantity demanded by the next production stage.

Pull System

Pull system is when each stage can pick the task when it's ready for the job. Unlike Push system, work or inventory is not pushed to the next level. It is achieved using the Kanban cards. 'Kanban' is a Japanese word for 'Signboard,' means 'message.' In 1940, Taiichi Ohno invented Kanban to achieve Just-in-time production, inspired by Supermarket model. In Supermarket model, the store inventory is maintained just to meet customer demand and restocked when it reaches a minimum level. Similarly, in Toyota, the inventory would be restocked only when there is Kanban Card available i.e. visual signal is there.

Kanban cards are a series of the colored cards which denote product details i.e. quantity and specification. A card placed in the container as a reference for next processing step. Details on Kanban card updated as per customer demand.

Another application of Kanban mostly in the Service Industry is to make a visual aid to maintain the list of activities at the various stage like 'Not Started,' 'In Progress' and 'Completed.' It can be an online dashboard or offline whiteboards. The major advantage of Kanban is that it maintains continuous flow without the need to maintain high inventory. Also, it is the best tool when the production priorities are dynamic. For example, in Kanban Software, if supervisor changes task priority, it will be visible to all stakeholder, and they can start working accordingly

Jidoka

Jidoka refers to the automation with a human touch. In 1896, Sakichi Toyoda, Founder of Toyota invented an automatic loom for weaving textiles. The loom would stop as soon as the thread broke, hence preventing the production of a defective product. As per lean guidelines, the defects should be identified and corrected at the earliest stage of production even if that means stopping production line. It helps in reducing the cost of poor quality and ensure defect-free production. Also, one person can manage multiple machines/processes as the machine/process stops when an error occurs, hence improving efficiency.

Heijunka

Heijunka is the Japanese word for 'Production smoothing' also known as production leveling, which means working and producing the same amount with consistency.

The parameter to consider while implementing production leveling is:

- Fluctuation in demand: As the customer demand is fluctuating, it is important to analyze the demand pattern and accordingly plan capacity
- Capacity Planning: Resources required is the function of cycle time and customer demand. Ensure cycle time is optimum.
- Resource allocation: Appropriate support available to meet the demand.
- Employee's skillset varies as per task type. Hence cross train employees if possible to reduce the cost to hire additional resources

Standardize Work

Standardized work means documenting the most efficient way of doing work which is also ergonomically correct and balanced. Standardized work is easily most underestimated Lean tool, but if implemented in right spirit it helps in maintaining productivity, quality, and safety.

There are three main elements to standardized work:

- Synchronizing Takt and Cycle time: Cycle time is the actual time required to process an order. Cycle time should be less than takt time to meet customer demand. In standardized work practice, the team should try to complete all orders within required takt time by standardizing work instructions. If there is major fluctuation in the cycle time of operators that means either the best practices are not adequately documented or not shared or not being followed. Well documented work instruction ensures a predictable outcome.
- Work Sequence: The sequence of work instruction should be defined to ensure ergonomic effectiveness. You should consider the work course while designing the plant/office layout. If required, the office or facility design should be changed to ensure efficient work sequencing.
- In-Process Stock: The stock level should be as low as possible to avoid the waste in the process. Standardized work ensures the stock level is maintained at a minimum level to achieve the normal operation.

Kaizen

'Kaizen' is a Japanese word. 'Kai' means 'better' and 'Zen' means 'change,' together it means 'Change for betterment.' Kaizen is a practice of continuous improvement.

TPS expect employees to follow standardized work guidelines and seek continual improvement. Since the inherent inefficiencies or problems in any procedure are most apparent to those closest to the process, hence members and team leader are the best to recommend Kaizen.

Lean Six Sigma

As discussed so far, Six Sigma focus on reducing variation in the process while the Lean concentrate on reducing waste. Both the methodologies are trying to reduce defect and improve efficiency. Hence there is a very blur line that divides these two philosophies. The consultants trained in both the methods, started to draw synergies, and hence the concept of Lean Six Sigma was introduced.

Lean uses more non-technical tools like Just-in-time, Pull System, Visual managements to achieve improvement while Six Sigma involves the application of statistical methods like Standard deviation, Hypothesis Testing, and Design of the experiments. Naturally, both the approaches have its inherent strength and weakness. Lean Six Sigma attempts to minimize weakness and leverage on strengths.

DMAIC

Edward Deming has consolidated Six Sigma methodology in five step model widely known as DMAIC, (Define, Measure, Analysis, Improve, and Control), which continued for Lean Six Sigma as well.

Define

Define helps to create the project outline, hence considered as the most critical stage of a six sigma project. The project results depend largely on how effectively scope is defined. The primary objective of this phase is to ensure the right problem is targeted. The project leader should ensure that the project has clear purpose and scope.

Following criteria should be considered before defining project objective.

- Six Sigma is the right methodology (both problem and solution are unknown)
- The data is available for analysis
- Leadership supports and approves project objective

The output of the Define phase is the project charter that includes goal statement (Project CTQ), scope, team charter and expected benefit.

Measure

Measure phase objective is to baseline the current performance of the process. At the end of this phase, the team should have following clarity:

- **Detailed process map**

In Define phase, we define the start and end of the process, and in Measure phase, the team should draw the detailed as-is process. The idea is to understand the current gaps. You should not incorporate any recommendation in process map at this stage.

- **Operation definition of the CTQ (Project 'Y') and Data Collection Plan**

  Measure phase will help to find answers for how, when, where and what exactly needs to capture. Sometimes data is readily available, but if not in the desired format, the team will have to recollect data.

- **Validated Measurement System**

  All measurement system requires calibration before utilization. The objective is to build a reliable measurement system

- **Performance Baseline**

  Once the data is collected, it is important to baseline the existing performance. Six Sigma being data driven process, various statistical tools used to baseline data.

Analyze

Till measure phase, the focus is on defining and baselining project metrics. In Analyze phase, the focus is to identify controllable root-causes which dictate variation in project parameters. The process input can be monitored and controlled to ensure desired value of project parameters achieved

Analyze phase is divided into two parts:

- Identification of root-causes (Xs)
- Validating root-causes

At the end of Analyze phase, the team should have finalized list of Xs that are statistically validated as well.

Improve

Once all the major root-causes of variation and waste are shortlisted, the team should brainstorm the solutions. The team can use various brainstorming, creative and Lean methods to identify required solutions. Once all the solutions are listed down team should conduct a cost-benefit analysis to finalize the improvement plan.

Control

This stage is probably the most ignored stage of the six sigma methodology. Once proposed solutions implemented, the team start working on other problem, but it is of utmost importance to ensure sustenance of the improvements. Hence a control plan is needed. A control plan should have documented solutions and escalation plan to manage performance fluctuation. In most of the practical scenarios, a six sigma project considered as complete, it the benefits is stable for minimum six months. However, the duration may vary as per company's requirement.

Part 2: Define

Project identification

Prioritization and Selection of Improvement Opportunity

In an organization, there are more improvement opportunities than what we can solve at a time. Hence it is important to prioritize opportunities. If your company doesn't already have defined criteria to select projects then basic tools like payoff matrix, criteria rating or failure mode effect analysis can be used. Following parameter should be considered while prioritizing a project:

1. Voice of customer and stakeholders
2. Key performance indicators
3. Company mission and vision
4. Time and ease to complete each project
5. Black Belt, Green Belt, and divisional resources.

Balance Scorecard

Balance scorecard is the strategic performance management tool, used to concisely present the company's performance on financial and non-financial parameters. The balanced scorecard is based on the research done by Robert Kaplan and David P. Norton.

It covers both leading and lagging indicators across four areas: financial, customer, internal process and employee learning. Balance scorecard is ideal for selecting six sigma project metrics (Y) as it includes the clients and business performance indicators.

Financial: "What are financial measures that are relevant to customers and stakeholders?" Examples: cash flow, sales growth, operating income, return on equity.

Customer: "What is important for our clients and stakeholders?" Examples: percent of sales from new products, on time delivery, the share of valuable customers' purchases, ranking by significant clients.

Internal business processes: "What do we need to do well internally to meet our customer goals, which will impact our financial standing?" Examples: cycle time, unit cost, yield, new product introductions.

Learning and growth: "How can we continue to improve, create value and innovate?" Examples: time to develop a new generation of products, life cycle to product maturity, time to market versus competition.

Critical to Quality

Introduction to CTQ

Critical to Quality (CTQ) is a measurable characteristic of the process/service or product which defines if the output is acceptable to the customer or not. For example, the temperature of the coffee, unless it's hot the client will not accept it, assuming he ordered hot coffee.

CTQ is an important term used in Lean Six Sigma projects. Obviously, for a product, there will be many CTQs. But for a six sigma project, one CTQ should be finalized to improve.

Key Performance Indicator

Key Performance Indicator or KPI is the commonly used terminology in a company. KPIs are the measures that demonstrate the performance of a company. Each process has their own KPIs which should align with overall company's goal. These KPIs are the project metrics i.e. Y for a six sigma project. Below is the list of common KPIs.

Lead Time:

Lead time is the time required to complete one order from the time it was placed

For example, if order placed at 14-Jan, 12:30 PM and delivered at 14-Jan, 2:30 PM,

$Lead\ time = Order\ Delivery\ Time - Order\ placed\ time$

$= 2:30\ PM - 12:30\ PM = 2\ hours$

Cycle Time

Cycle time is the time spent in executing required task. In the previous example, the order was placed at 12:30 PM but resource start working on order only at 1:30 PM. This one hour waiting time (12:30 to 1:30 PM) is included in calculating lead time but not cycle time.

$Cycle\ time = Processing\ time = 2:30\ PM - 1:30\ PM = 1\ hour$

Lead time is always be greater than or equal to cycle time. The smaller the difference between lead time and cycle time, better the efficiency of the process.

Takt time

Takt time is the rate at which order should be produced to meet customer demand with available resources.

Continuing with the earlier example, let's assume:

Employee working in team = 10; Working Day per week = 5 Days; Working Hours (Productive time) per day = 8 hours

$$Total\ Productive\ Time = 10 * 5 * 8 = 400\ hours$$

$$Max\ Production/week = \frac{Total\ Productive\ time}{Lead\ time} = \frac{400}{2} = 200$$

The existing setup can fulfill customer demand that is less than the maximum possible production i.e 200 orders.

However, let's assume, customer demand for a week is 250 orders. Then,

$$Takt\ time = \frac{Total\ Prodcutive\ time}{Customer\ demand} = \frac{400\ hours}{250\ order} = 1.6\ hours\ per\ order$$

This means we have 1.6 hours to process one order.

Lead time should always be less than takt time to meet customer demand.

Change-Over time

Change over time is the time required by machine or process to change from a state of producing one type of product to another.

As there is no output generated during the change-over period, smaller the change over time better the process efficiency.

Availability Time

It is the available productive time of the machine or process. For example, a machine is running for 8 hours per day and is functional only on weekdays, so the available time per week is 40 hours (8 hours per day * 5 days). However, in a particular week, if there is 5 hr. planned downtime for the machine, the availability time for that week is 35 hours (40-5).

Utilization

Utilization is the percentage of productive time spent in processing. For example, out of 80 hours available for process ABC, because of low volume, only 60 hours is spent in processing order. That means.

$$Utilization = \frac{\text{\# Hours spend in production}}{Available\ time} * 100$$

$$= \frac{60\ hours}{80\ hours} * 100 = 75\ \%$$

This means Process ABC still has an unfulfilled capacity of 25% which can be used to process additional volume or take up additional responsibility.

Productivity

Productivity is the amount of output (goods or services) produced per labor hours i.e. it is the ratio of output divided by input. For example, if 200 transactions are processed per week by 5 resources. Assuming 8 productive hours per resource per day,

$$Productivity = \frac{200}{(5*8)} = 5\ Tranaction\ per\ hour$$

If a company is planning to improve productivity, this means they want to achieve more output with the same number of resources.

Efficiency

Efficiency is often confused with productivity. Efficiency is achieving same with less input. For example, if company targets to improve efficiency, this means they want to reduce the number of resources to achieve the same output.

Efficiency is more relevant than productivity in most of the scenario, as output is customer driven. Considering the previous example, if every week, the customer is raising only 200 tickets, then productivity cannot be improved over 5 transactions per day. However, the efficiency can be improved.

Defects per unit

Defects per unit is the average number of defect found per unit.

$$Defects\ per\ unit\ (DPU) = \frac{\#\ Defects\ found\ in\ all\ units}{Total\ units\ processed}$$

Defects per million opportunity

The product or service can have multiple opportunities for error (OFE). For example in a mobile phone, microphone, speaker, camera, overall body, etc. are opportunities for error. Each one of them will be considered as a defect if not met the client expectation.

$Defects\ per\ million\ opportunity\ (DPMO)$

$$= \left[\frac{\#\ Defects\ found\ in\ all\ units}{(Total\ units\ processed) * (\#Opportunities\ of\ error)}\right] * 1000{,}000$$

OEE

OEE or Overall Equipment Efficiency is used in the manufacturing industry to measure the performance of a manufacturing unit. It takes into consideration Availability/Uptime, Performance, and Quality of the machine.

$$OEE = Availability * Performance * Quality$$

$$Availability = \frac{Expected\ available\ time - Downtime}{Expected\ available\ time}$$

$$Performance = \frac{Actual\ Production}{Maximum\ possible\ Production\ capacity}$$

$$Quality = \frac{Defect\ free\ units\ produced}{Total\ units\ produced}$$

It is tough to achieve 100% OEE, which means machine was up for 100% time, running at its highest speed and producing all defect free products. Most of the company's target for 80-85% of OEE.

First Pass Yield and Rolled Throughput Yield

First Pass Yield (FPY) is the percentage of units produced defect free in first attempts. For example, 300 units produced, out of which 250 could pass the inspection and 50 had to go through rework. Post rework, 45 could pass inspection and 5 had to be scrapped.

$$FPY = \frac{250}{300} = 83\%,$$

The 45 units which have passed inspection post rework are not included in the FPY calculation.

Now if there are three process steps for one production unit, the Rolled Throughput Yield (RTY) is calculated for the overall production unit.

$$RTY = FTY1 * FTY2 * FTY3$$

Assuming each process step has first pass yield on 75%.

$$RTY = 75\% * 75\% * 75\% = 42\%$$

Only 42% of units are produced correctly in the first attempt by this production unit.

Attrition Rate

Attrition rate is a percentage of resources leaving the organization.

$$Attrition\ rate = \frac{Number\ of\ employees\ left\ organization\ in\ a\ month}{Team\ Size}$$

There are two types of attrition:

1. Voluntary Attrition is when employee decided to leave the company
2. Involuntary Attrition is when employer ask employee to leave the organization

Timelines

Timelines is the percentage of output delivered as per timelines agreed with client for a given period

$$Timelines = \frac{Number\ of\ transactions\ completed\ on\ time}{Total\ transactions\ completed}$$

Voice of Customer

In today's competitive world, the customer has multiple options to choose for a product. The strategies that are customer driven have proven market leaders across all sectors. With limited resources available, it is crucial for the organization to decide where to invest for achieving maximum benefits.

Six Sigma project takes lots of work and gives maximum benefit if used to solve the problem that is important for business. Hence, the project ideas that are customer focused has always given long-term business benefit.

The customer is anyone who is ready to pay for the output. The customer can either be internal to the organization like other team, employees, etc. or external to the organization like client or end users.

The customer expectations can either be stated or unstated; different methodologies should be used to capture the voice of the customer.

1. **Feedback**: Quickest and simplest way to understand customer need is by listening to customer feedback or suggestion. However, Feedbacks can be vague and require proper drill down to get to the problem statement. For example, "Process is not performing as per expectation." First, understand what the expectation is, then the gap analysis can be done. Another example can be "Process efficiency has not improved in last few year." The right question to ask is "How much

improvement was expected, 10%, 20% or anything else?"

2. **Surveys**: A questionnaire can be called upon to understand customer needs. Surveys should be designed with caution to ensure it is short at the same time cover all essential points. The response rate for surveys is in general low, but for long reviews, it is even lower.
3. **Focused Group**: A discussion with a group of relevant stakeholder on the predefined topic can also help in understanding customer expectation. Focused group discussion should be moderated to ensure team stick to the point, and all the participants get to contribute.
4. **Meetings**: The weekly or monthly discussion with the client gives many pointers if observed carefully. Customer tends to share pain areas or other observations/concerns that can act as the voice of the customer.

Kano Model

Noriaki Kano developed a model to explain the relationship between customer satisfaction and quality. As per Kano, there are three levels of quality of a product or services:

1. **Basic Quality**: These are essential features in a product or service, which if not met cause dissatisfaction, but the mere presence does not create a satisfied customer.

   For example, the messaging (SMS) feature in the mobile phone, if not available cause resentment, but the availability does not ensure that consumer is happy with the phone.

2. **Expected Quality**: These functions are the ones which if not present cause dissatisfaction and if available increases the satisfaction level of the customer.

   For example, mobile phone camera specifications as the pixels increased so as the client satisfaction level but of course after some time expected quality would slowly move to basic quality level. In the 90s, 5 MP camera for a mobile phone was a privilege, but now it's essential requirement.

3. **Expected Quality**: These are unexpected features in product or services that increase customer satisfaction if present but won't cause

dissatisfaction if absent. For example, front camera in mobile, when first introduced.

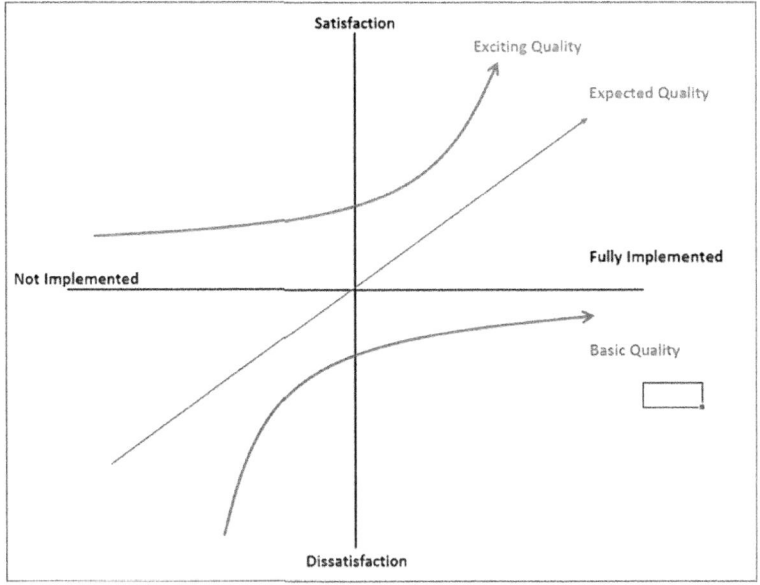

Figure 4: Kano Model

Over a period, the exciting feature moves to expected and expected moves to basic. Hence, the organization must continuously try to understand the different level of customer expectations.

Project Charter

The project charter is the one-page document which gives a summary of the six sigma project. Define phase can be signed off if all the required parameters captured in the charter.

Project charter elements:

1. Process Overview
2. Problem Statement
3. Project Goal
4. Project Scope
5. Team Charter
6. Project Timelines
7. Expected Benefit

Project Charter: *Name*			
Process Overview	Scope		
	In Scope		Out of Scope
Problem Statement	Team Charter		
	Champion		
	Master Black Belt		
	Black Belt		
	Green Belt		
Goal	Team Member 1		
	Team Member 2		
	Team Member 3		
	Team Member 4		
	Timelines		
Expected Benefit	Define		
	Measure		
	Analyze		
	Improve		
	Control		

Figure 5: Project Charter

Project Goal

The project goal should be SMART (Specific, Measurable, Achievable, Relevant and Time-bound).

Specific: The goal should be clearly defined so that everyone can understand

Measurable: It should be measurable to follow the progress of the project

Achievable: It is nice to have an inspirational goal, but it should also be practical to achieve. Changing the direction of a big vehicle takes more time compared to smaller one. Similarly, organizational parameters should be kept in account while setting a goal.

Realistic: The goal can be achieved with the available resources

Time-Based: The project timelines should be finalized considering the time required to reach the target.

The project goal should give clear guidance on how much improvement on the project metrics (Y) performance is expected from the team in the specified timelines.

SIPOC

SIPOC is one of the best scoping tools, stands for Supplier, Input, Process, Output, and Customer. SIPOC displays process activities along with end-to-end flow from supplier to customer.

Supplier: Entity that provides input for processing

Input: Information or document required to execute the process

Process: Set of activities that if implemented in a particular sequence generates value for customer

Output: Final or work-in-progress output deliverables that either shared with client or used to execute next process step

Customer: Customer is the one who will use the output

While creating an SIPOC, start with 'P' block, and write all the process steps at high-level that shows the flow. Ideally, SIPOC should not have more than ten process steps. If there are more than ten steps, you should break SIPOCs into two.

Once SIPOC is created, decide on what is the scope of the project.

- Scope should not be too narrow or too broad
- Clearly define what is in scope or out of scope
- It should cover problem statement
- Sponsor should have control over scope area

Team Charter

Six Sigma project is a team effort. The roles and responsibilities for the project are carefully designed by considering the size and time required to execute the project, as discussed below.

Champion

- Part of management team of the organization selects and approves project charter
- Conduct regular project review
- Responsible for clearing the roadblocks of the project

Master Black Belt

- Responsible for ensuring six sigma methodology followed in right spirit
- Train Black Belts on the six sigma guidelines, mentor project if required

Black Belt

- Black belt responsible for training process stakeholders on six sigma guidelines
- Support in all statistical analysis
- Support cross functional execution and facilitate all discussion

- Conduct reviews with the champion and green belts

Green Belt

- Green belt is responsible for executing and completing project
- Finalize other team members for the project
- Define scope and goal with champion
- Work in close collaboration with Black Belt to conduct required statistical analysis
- Ensure proposed solutions implemented
- Track sustenance of improvement in control phase
- Handover project to process owner once completed

Team Members

- The team members for the project should represent different skill sets and functions
- They help in achieving project target by providing required inputs at various stage.

ARMI Model

ARMI model is a tool to define roles and responsibilities of project members at a different stage. ARMI stands for:

A - Approval

R – Resource (who executes)

M – Members (provide inputs)

I - Interested Party, (need to be informed on the progress)

Below shows the ARMI model for Six Sigma project.

	Define	Measure	Analyze	Improve	Control
Champion	A	A	A	A	A
Master Black Belt	A	A	A	A	A
Black Belt	A	A	A	A	A
Green Belt	R	R	R	R	R
Team Member	M	M	M	R	M
Customer	I	I	I	I	I

Figure 6: ARMI Model

Part 3: Measure

Data Types

Continuous and Discrete data are two main categories of data.

Continuous data is the data that can express in the form of fractions. For example, temperature, height or percentage, etc. Even between 1 and 2, there can be infinite observations like 1.0009, 1.0000009, etc.

Discrete data, on the other hand, can only express as the whole number i.e. can take limited values. For example, a number of defectives produced, it can be either 2 or 3, can't be 2.5. Discrete data sometimes also referred as **attribute data** as it is used to calculate attributes of a product.

Discrete data is further categorized as:

1. **Nominal data** is captured in categories and does not have any natural order.
   For example, male and female in a city, geographical location, marital status.
2. **Ordinal data** is similar to nominal data but does have original order.
   For example, customer satisfaction ranked from 1 to 5, '1' being most satisfied. However, level 2

doesn't mean the client is twice as happy as listed at level 1.

3. **Count data** is when the occurrences of an even captured. For example, the number of transactions executed daily.

Continuous data is always preferred over discrete data as

- ✓ Continuous data is more accurate than discrete data
- ✓ Few samples of continuous data are sufficient to conduct statistical analysis.

You can convert discrete data into continuous data by calculating the percentage, called as pseudo-continuous data. For example, 20 products are defective out of 100 produced. The defective count is a discrete data but defect rate i.e. the percentage of errors 20% (20/100) is a continuous data.

Basic Statistics

Measure of central tendency

Central tendency refers to the location of the data i.e. the tendency of data to cluster around a particular value. Central tendency is measured using Mean, Median, and Mode.

Mean

Mean is the arithmetical average of the data i.e. division of the sum of data points by the number of data points.

$$\overline{Y} = \frac{Y_1 + Y_2 + \ldots + Y_n}{n}$$

For example, for data set 1, 2, 3, 4, 5:

$$Mean = \frac{1+2+3+4+5}{5} = \frac{15}{5} = 3$$

Mean gives the location of dataset i.e. for the above data set 1, 2, 3, 4, 5, the center is '3' i.e. most of the data points are centered in and around 3.

Though mean is the simplest way to summarize data, it is influenced by the extreme numbers in the set.

For example, the average of '1, 2, 3, 4, 5' and '1, 0, 8' is 3. Hence you can't use mean all alone to summarize data.

Mode

Mode is the most frequently occurred data point in the set.

For example, for a dataset 1, 2, 2, 3, 4, 5; mode is '2' because there are two observations of '2'.

Not all the data sets will have a mode. For example, dataset '1, 2, 3, 4, 5' doesn't have mode as all the numbers have occurred only once.

Median

Median is the center of the data set when arranged in ascending/descending order.

For example, '1, 2, 6, 7, 3, 4, 1, 6, 8' is the data set.

To find median first, arrange data in ascending order '1, 1, 2, 3, 4, 6, 6, 7, 8'. Here, '4' is the Median.

For an even number of data set like '1, 2, 3, 4', the median is an average of middle two numbers i.e. 2.5 (average of 2 and 3).

Quartile

The median divide data into two equal parts i.e. 50% of the data is on either side of the median, known as the second quartile (Q_2). Similarly, there is first (Q_1) and third (Q_3) quartile.

The first quartile (Q_1) divides data into two part such as 25% of the observations are less than Q_1 and 75% more than Q_1.

The third quartile (Q_3) is a data point when 75% of data is less than and 25% of data is more than Q_3.

Kurtosis

Kurtosis is the measure of the degree of peakedness of the data. Kurtosis value can either be positive or negative; zero indicates that the data distribution is normal. The high positive value indicates the data is sharper than the normal peak while negative data indicates data is flatter than the normal.

Skewness

Skewness refers to the degree to which data is not symmetric. Skewness is zero when data is equally distributed around the center value, i.e., the mean is equal to the median.

Positive skewness is when the data is focused on lower value and tail is towards the right. Negative skewness has tail towards left i.e. most of the data points is centered on higher value.

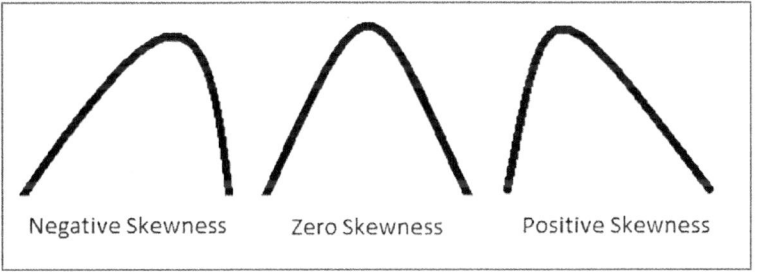

Negative Skewness   Zero Skewness   Positive Skewness

Figure 7: Skewness

Measure of dispersion

The measure of dispersion is used to understand the spread of data. There are three measures used to calculate the data spread.

Range

'Range' is the difference between largest and smallest value of the data set.

Consider below example showing average handling time in minutes for 15 transactions.

Transaction Number	1	2	3	4	5	6	7	8	9	10
Average Handling time (min)	109	149	110	142	124	115	131	134	133	121

Figure 8: Average handling time

Lowest value = 109

Largest value = 149

Range = 149-109 = 40

That means the maximum possible difference between two average handling times (AHT) is 40 minutes.

Variance and Standard Deviation

The range tells that AHT is fluctuating between 109 min to 149 min but won't explain the spread of data around mean.

Variance and standard deviation can illustrate the data fluctuation around mean.

Variance is the average difference of data points from the mean. As the sum of difference of data points from mean will be zero, to calculate variance, we take a square of difference.

$$Variance\ for\ sample(s^2) = \sum_{i}^{n} \frac{(Yi - \bar{Y})^2}{(n-1)}$$

$$Variance\ for\ pupulation(\sigma^2) = \sum_{i}^{n} \frac{(Yi - \bar{Y})^2}{(n)}$$

$$Standard\ deviation\ for\ sample = s = \sqrt{s^2}$$

$$Standard\ deviation\ for\ population = \sigma = \sqrt{\sigma^2}$$

Data Collection Planning

The soul of a six sigma project is data. In few scenarios, data is readily available in the required form. But if not available, data collection planning becomes crucial.

The operational definition of CTQ is the clear description of the parameter which can be used to collect data. For example, there are multiple ways to capture temperature of a room. If a thermometer is placed right below air conditioner, the result will be different than if the temperature captured at the corner of the room. Hence, it is important to give clear guidelines on the measurement methodology.

Operation definition of CTQ includes following parameters:

- CTQ: a measurable parameter that team is trying to improve i.e. Project Y. For example, cycle time.
- Data Type: Continuous or discrete data
- Unit of Measure: For example, is it hours, minutes or second for average handling time?
- Specifications: Upper and lower specification limits given by client that is acceptable for a product or services
- Target: The expected performance level for Y
- Data Source: From where the data will be collected?

- Data collection method: How are we going to collect data? For example, Time when advisor closes the request on the tool post resolving minus time when a client raises request on the tool.
- Data collection frequency: Data will be captured every hour, daily, monthly or yearly?
- Sample Size: All data points i.e. population or a small set of data i.e. sample will be considered for statistical analysis?

Sampling

The population is the entire set of data under consideration, while the sample is the portion of data that fairly represents the data set. For example, to understand the opinion of women on an advertisement, asking each woman of the country or state is time-consuming and costly, hence sample of data is collected.

Sample Type

There are two types of samples, non-random and random sample.

Non-random Sample

The sample is collected as per personal knowledge & opinion of the experts. Though the non-random sample is convenient to collect and is cost effective, the inferences of the non-random sample cannot be generalized as they are biased and doesn't represent overall population.

Random or Probability Sample

In the probability sample, all items have an equal chance of being selected. There are four types of random samples.

1. **Simple random sample**: Items are picked up randomly. For example, numbers generated by the computer. For a simple random sample, each item has equal chance to pick.
2. **Systematic Sample**: The first item is selected using simple random sampling after that next item is systematically selected as predefined. For example, take feedback from every seventh person entering the store. The first person is randomly picked, and then every seventh person is asked to give feedback.
3. **Stratified Sample**: The population is divided into sub-population or strata according to common characteristics, for example, time, space, gender, etc. The simple random sample then picked up from the strata. In the end, the results from each stratum are combined to derive population behavior.
4. **Cluster Sample**: The population is divided into naturally occurring subdivision like countries, families, etc. then the simple random sample is picked up from that.

Sample Size for random sample

Bigger the sample size better the accuracy but collecting sample size required time, effort and money hence it should be a fair balance of both.

$$\text{Sample Size for continuous data} = \left[\frac{Z_{1-\alpha/2} \times \sigma}{\Delta}\right]^2$$

α: Error allowed in the sample (generally considered as 5%)

σ: Standard deviation of the population

Δ: Interval in which the population mean needs to be estimated

For discrete data,

$$\text{Standard deviation } (\sigma) = \sqrt{p(1-p)}$$

p: Population proportion of non-defectives

Hence,

$$\text{Sample Size for discrete data} = \left[\frac{Z_{1-\alpha/2}}{\Delta}\right]^2 \times p(1-p)$$

Measurement System Analysis

Six Sigma practitioner mostly skips Measurement System Analysis (MSA), but it is important to understand variation in the measurement system. The objective of MSA is to study measurement system finalize one with a minimum acceptable error.

Measurement system included anything that can affect the measurement of the data i.e. equipment or application (Gage) used and operator involved etc.

Measurement System Characteristics

The measurement system can be defined using Accuracy and Precision.

Accuracy

Accuracy defines how close observed value is to the true value, i.e. if a person's weight is 53.2 kg, the digital weighing machine should show 53.2 kg, not 53.0 or 53.7 kg.

The accuracy of a measurement system is calculated using:

1. **Bias:** The difference between actual value and the measured value

2. **Linearity**: The difference in the bias through the range of measurements. Linearity is basically how accurate gage is measuring throughout the reference value. Linearity is calculated to ensure gage has the same accuracy across all reference value

Precision

Precision defines how effectively the same result can be produced again.

Variation in measurement system can be classified into two categories:

1. **Repeatability**: Variation due to gage
2. **Reproducibility:** Variation due to the operator

Reproducibility can be because of:

- Variation in measurement of same part by different operator
- Variation in measurement by different operator/part combination

Below figure shows all possible scenarios for accuracy and precision. If the measurement system is not accurate, the requirement is to shift the mean of the system, and if it is not precise, team has to work on adjusting the deviation

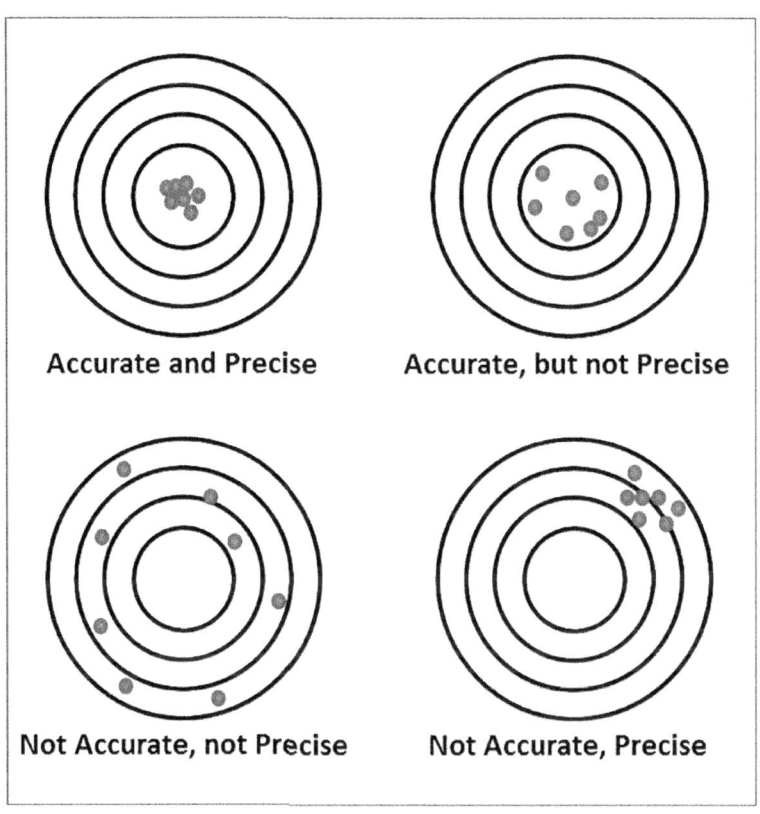

Figure 9: Accuracy and Precision

Depending on the data type, the gage R&R studies can be used to evaluate the measurement system characteristics.

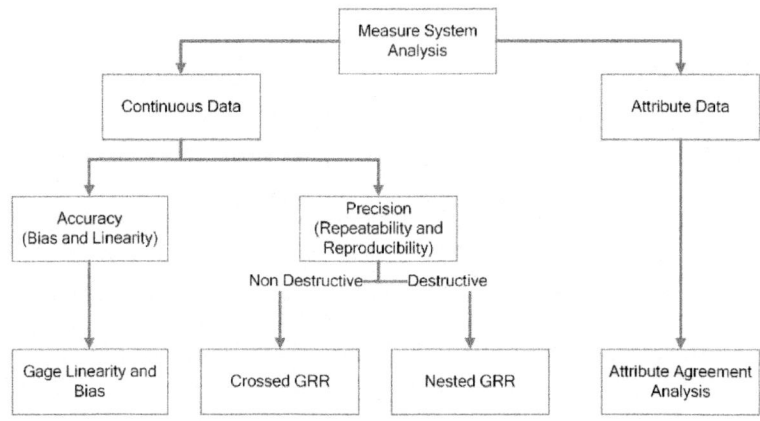

Figure 10: MSA Flowchart

Gage Linearity and Bias

Gage Linearity and Bias Study is used for assessing the accuracy of continuous data measurement system.

For example, a gage is used to measure five different parts whose reference values (actual diameter measurement) are 2, 4, 6, 8 and 10 centimeters. The reading of the various trials for each part is maintained as below.

Part	Reference	Reading
1	2	2.10
1	2	2.02
1	2	2.03
1	2	2.01
1	2	1.94
1	2	2.06

Figure 11: Gage Linearity and Bias - Data input

Figure 12 shows the statistical software results of linearity and bias test.

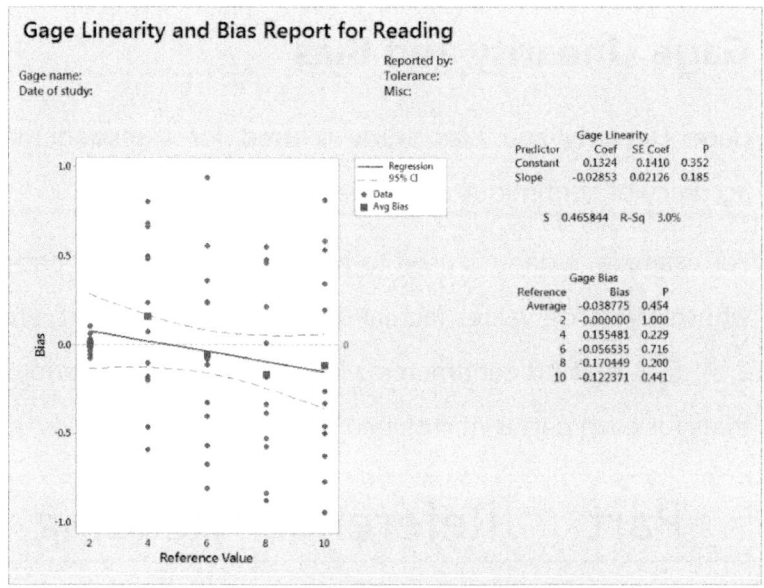

Figure 12: Gage Linearity and Bias

The average P value and corresponding P-value for each of the parts is greater than 0.05. Hence you can conclude the bias is insignificant in the measurement.

The slope of the line indicates if the linearity of the gage is significant or not, P-value greater than 0.05 indicates even the linearity is acceptable.

Note: The importance of P-value will be discussed in detailed in Hypothesis testing (as part of Analyze phase)

Gage Reproducibility and Repeatability (GR&R)

Gage R&R is the study conducted to calculate the acceptability of the measurement system. The various statistical software can be used to measure if the measurement system variation is small compared to the process variation and hence acceptable for usage. Also, it helps illustrate if repeatability and reproducibility of the gage are above the accepted levels.

There are different types of GR&R test depending on the data collection setup.

1. Crossed GR&R: Use when each operator measures each part multiple times (hence called as crossed).
2. Nested GR&R: Use when each operator measures individual part only once, mostly because the part is destroyed in the measurement process.
3. Extended GR&R: Use when one of the following conditions exists:
    a. Measurement system has more than two factors, usually operator, gage, and part
    b. Fixed or random factors
    c. Both crossed and nested factors

d. An unbalanced design

Let's consider a measurement system analysis where different operators are asked to measure the diameter of various parts.

As this is a non-destructive test for continuous data, crossed gage R&R study is applicable.

Figure 13 and 14 shows the output of a statistical software of the crossed gage R&R ANOVA analysis for a measurement system where operator A, B, C, D have measured the diameter of part 1, 2, 3, 4, and 5.

The reference values of part 1, 2, 3, 4, and 5 are 2, 4, 6, 8, and 10 cm respectively.

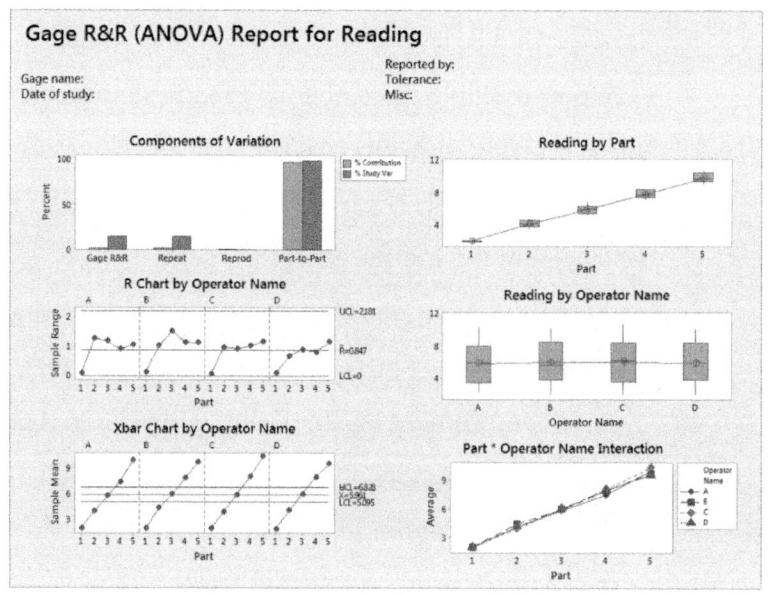

Figure 13: Crossed Gage R&R – ANOVA

Two-Way ANOVA Table With Interaction

```
Source              DF     SS       MS        F       P
Part                 4   453.374  113.344  702.547  0.000
Operator Nam         3     0.289    0.096    0.596  0.629
Part * Operator Nam 12     1.936    0.161    0.646  0.790
Repeatability       40     9.986    0.250
Total               59   465.585
```

α to remove interaction term = 0.05

Two-Way ANOVA Table Without Interaction

```
Source          DF     SS       MS        F       P
Part             4   453.374  113.344  494.358  0.000
Operator Nam     3     0.289    0.096    0.420  0.740
Repeatability   52    11.922    0.229
Total           59   465.585
```

Gage R&R

```
                                    %Contribution
Source              VarComp         (of VarComp)
Total Gage R&R      0.22927               2.37
  Repeatability     0.22927               2.37
  Reproducibility   0.00000               0.00
    Operator Nam    0.00000               0.00
Part-To-Part        9.42619              97.63
Total Variation     9.65547             100.00


                                    Study Var    %Study Var
Source              StdDev (SD)     (6 × SD)       (%SV)
Total Gage R&R       0.47883         2.8730         15.41
  Repeatability      0.47883         2.8730         15.41
  Reproducibility    0.00000         0.0000          0.00
    Operator Nam     0.00000         0.0000          0.00
Part-To-Part         3.07021        18.4213         98.81
Total Variation      3.10732        18.6439        100.00
```

Number of Distinct Categories = 9

Figure 14: Gage R&R (ANOVA) results

Measurement Acceptable?

The measurement system is acceptable when following range of % Contribution and % Study variation is met.

The % Contribution is the percentage of process variation from that source while % Study variation is calculated as 100 times the study variation for that source divided by the total study variation.

Measurement System is	% Contribution	% Study Var
Acceptable	<1%	<10%
Acceptable depending on the application, the cost of the measurement device, cost of repair, or other factors	Between 1% and 9%	Between 10% and 30%
Not Acceptable	Greater than 9%	Greater than 30%

•

Attribute Agreement Analysis

Attribute Agreement Analysis is used for attribute data to check if the ratings given by appraisers match the standards or not. This analysis is used to verify the accuracy of measurement system where the results as captured as good/bad or pass/fail.

Let's assume a measurement system analysis, where operator A, B, C, and D are asked to conduct a quality check for part 1, 2, 3, 4, and 5. The result of the check is Pass or Fail. The reference value of the quality check of all the five parts is already available with the team.

Figure 15 and 16 represents result of the attribute agreement analysis result of statistical software.

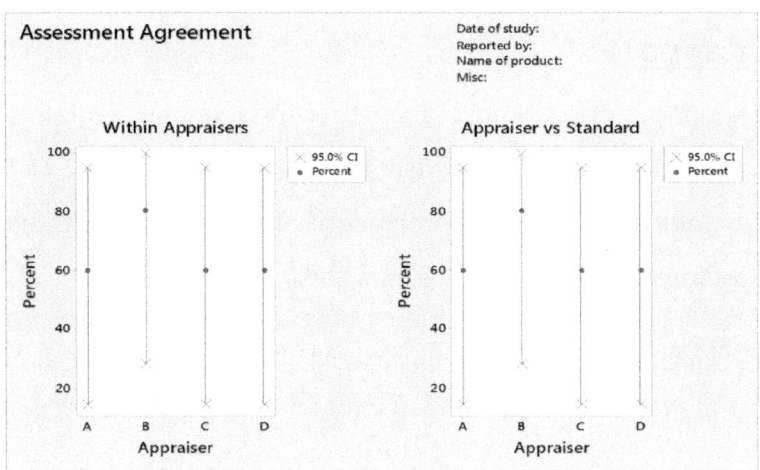

Figure 15: Attribute Data Analysis

```
Attribute Agreement Analysis for Reading

Within Appraisers

Assessment Agreement

Appraiser  # Inspected  # Matched  Percent      95% CI
A                   5          3    60.00  (14.66, 94.73)
B                   5          4    80.00  (28.36, 99.49)
C                   5          3    60.00  (14.66, 94.73)
D                   5          3    60.00  (14.66, 94.73)

# Matched: Appraiser agrees with him/herself across trials.


Fleiss' Kappa Statistics

Appraiser  Response     Kappa  SE Kappa        Z   P(vs > 0)
A          Fail      0.464286  0.258199  1.79817      0.0361
           Pass      0.464286  0.258199  1.79817      0.0361
B          Fail      0.732143  0.258199  2.83558      0.0023
           Pass      0.732143  0.258199  2.83558      0.0023
C          Fail      0.444444  0.258199  1.72133      0.0426
           Pass      0.444444  0.258199  1.72133      0.0426
D          Fail      0.444444  0.258199  1.72133      0.0426
           Pass      0.444444  0.258199  1.72133      0.0426
```

Figure 16: Attribute Agreement Analysis - Within Appraiser

Kappa

Kappa or Fleiss' Kappa Statistics measure the degree of agreement in the assessments. Its value varies from -1 to 1. 1 indicates perfect agreement, -1 indicates complete disagreement while 0 indicates 50:50 chances.

Kappa value of greater than 0.7 is considered safe.

P (vs>0)

P-value describes the chances of having a Fleiss Kappa near 0. Lower the value of P-value indicates lesser the likelihood of the Kappa values is 0 or less. If P-value is less than 0.05, then you can conclude that the appraiser's agreement is not due to chance. Hence we can conclude that the appraisers are either in agreement or disagreement with each other and standard.

Process Capability

There are two capability indices (Cp, Cpk) defined in statistics which can be utilized for continuous data or unit-less data.

C_p

Cp is calculated as the ratio of the customer specified tolerance limit to natural tolerance (6σ).

For a continuous normally distributed data, 6σ i.e. 3σ on either side of mean covers 99.67% of the data.

$$Cp = \frac{USL - LSL}{6\sigma}$$

$$Cp = 3 * Zst$$

For a six sigma process, there are six standard deviation on either side of mean within specification limit,

Hence, USL = 6σ and LSL = -6σ

So,

$$Cp = \frac{6\sigma - (-6\sigma)}{6\sigma} = \frac{12\sigma}{6\sigma} = 2$$

Cp should be greater than '1' to ensure the process is meeting customer specification.

The issue with Cp is that it does not take into account the location of data i.e. mean, only the spread is taken into consideration.

For a process, if Cp is greater than 1, it is possible that none of the products are meeting specification as the performance is not located at the required location.

C_{pk}

Unlike Cp, Cpk takes location as well as spread into consideration.

$$Cpk = Min\left[\frac{USL - \overline{X}}{3\sigma}, \frac{\overline{X} - LSL}{3\sigma}\right]$$

Cpk greater than 1.33 is the ideal condition but even greater than 1 is acceptable capability.

A process is called capable when it is performing within specification limit (given by client) and is referred as stable when the performance is within +/- 3σ i.e. fluctuating within 3 standard deviation level. Control charts are used to check if the process is stable.

Sigma Level

Sigma level indicates the compliance rate of the process i.e. how effective process in avoiding defect or in other words is meeting client's expectation. It is considered to be the positive way of representing the process capability

Short Term Sigma Level (Z_{st})

Short term sigma level is calculated using within standard deviation of the process. Z_{st} represents the potential capability of the process i.e. how the process will perform if all short term variations are constant which is an ideal scenario.

Long Term Sigma Level (Z_{st})

Long term sigma level is calculated using the overall process standard deviation, hence representing the actual capability of the process. It is considered that over the period because of natural variation the short term sigma level is shifted by 1.5σ. Thus Z_{LT} can also be calculated as

$$Z_{LT} = Z_{st} - 1.5$$

Sigma level can be calculated for both attribute data as well as continuous data.

Sigma Level for Attribute data

The sigma level for discrete data is calculated using DPU and DPMO.

$$Defects\ per\ unit\ (DPU) = \frac{Total\ number\ of\ defects\ found\ in\ all\ the\ units}{Total\ units\ processed}$$

Defects per million opportunity (DPMO)

$$= \left[\frac{\#Defects\ found\ in\ all\ the\ units}{(Total\ units\ processed) * (\#Opportunities\ of\ error)}\right] * 1000,000$$

The standard normal distribution (Z-distribution) is the tool referred to calculate the sigma level using DPMO.

Zlt (Long term sigma level)	Zst (Short term Sigma Level)	DPMO
1	2.5	158655.25
1.5	3	66807.20
2	3.5	22750.13
2.5	4	6209.67
3	4.5	1349.90
3.5	5	232.63
4	5.5	31.67
4.5	6	3.40

Figure 17: Sigma Level

Sigma Level for Continuous data

Sigma level for continuous data is represented as the number of standard deviations (σ) can fit between the

Mean and closest specification limit (SL). If Zst is six, that means six standard deviations (σ) can be accommodated between mean and SL. Higher Zst means lower the variation hence lower the DPMOs.

$$Z_{ST} = \frac{|SL - Mean|}{\sigma_{st}}$$

$$Z_{LT} = \frac{|SL - Mean|}{\sigma_{lt}}$$

Process Variation

Common and Special Variation

There are two types of variations observed in a process:

1. Common cause variation: These are inherent or natural variation in the process that are there irrespective of how effective the process is designed. The process is considered to be stable if it has only common cause variations.
2. Special cause variation: There are assignable causes, i.e. this variation is triggered externally and can be assigned to a particular event. If a process has special cause variation, it is said to be out-of-control.

There are various graphs available that can be used to represent the variation in the process.

Histogram

A Histogram is a graph representing the frequency of occurrence of data points in a particular interval.

For example, consider average handling time for a process captured for few transactions.

Transaction Number	1	2	3	4	5	6	7	8	9	10	11	12	13	14	15	16	17	18	19	20	21
Average Handling time (min)	108	101	107	108	103	110	106	101	106	107	109	104	103	107	102	104	108	109	107	110	106

<u>**Figure 18: Average Handling Time**</u>

Figure 19 represents the histogram of the data. A frequency polygon is constructed by connecting midpoints of the histogram bar as depicted by line graph (red line).

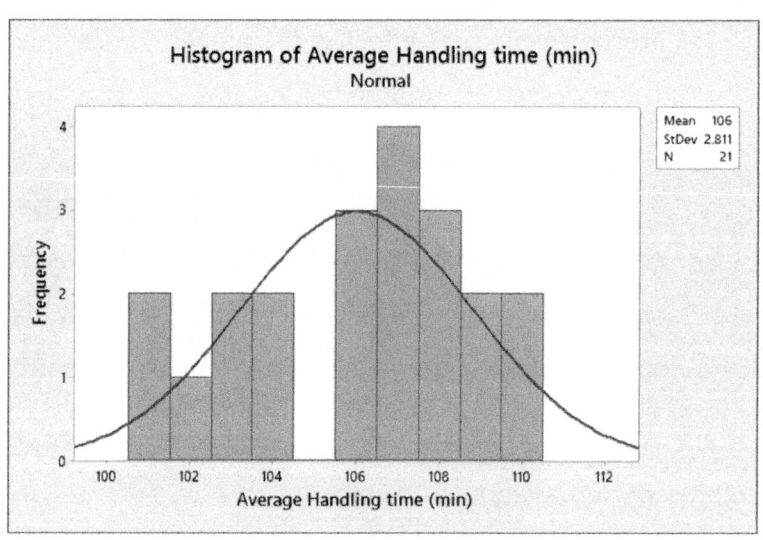

<u>**Figure 19: Histogram**</u>

Dot Plot

Dot plot similar to histogram used to illustrate the data distribution.

Figure 20 shows the Dot plot for average handling time.

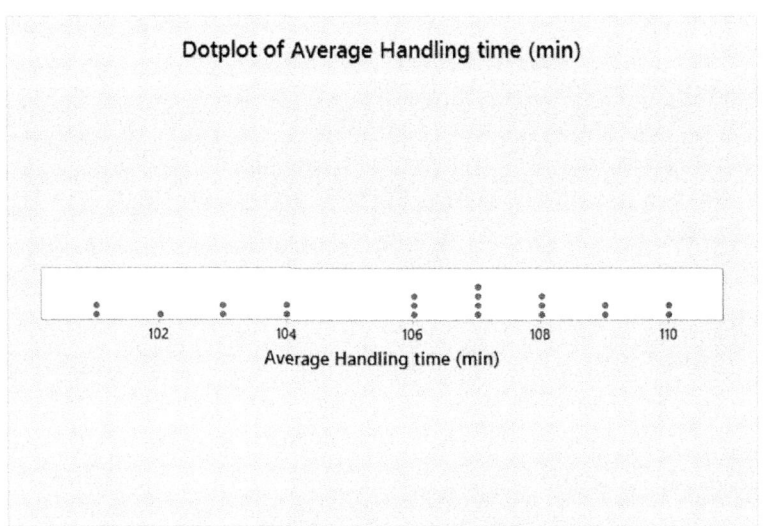

Figure 20: Dot plot

Box Plot

Box Plot is one of the most famous six sigma tool, used to identify the outliers in the database.

Figure 21 the box plot for the average handling time.

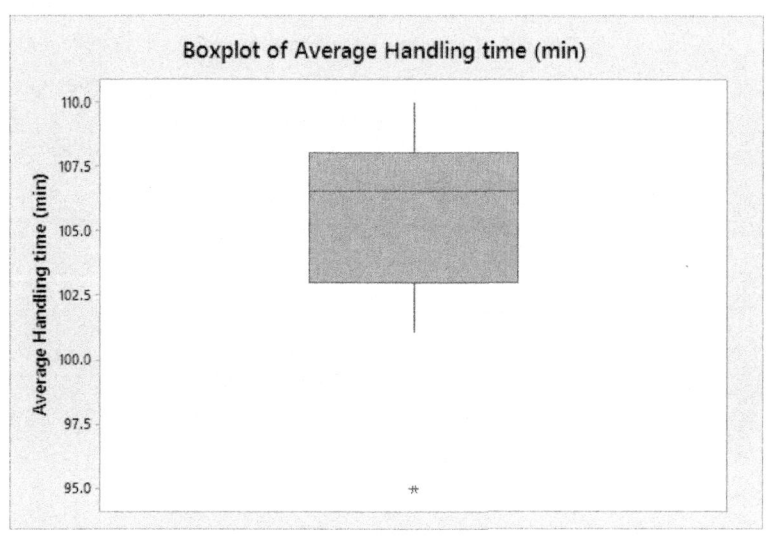

Figure 21: Box Plot with outlier

The box, in the graph, refers to the interquartile range (Q3-Q1), i.e. it represents 50% of the observation.

The lowest line of the box indicates first quartile Q1, middle line is the median (Q2), and top-most line refers to Q3

The vertical lines above and below the box are 'whisker.' The top most point of the upper whisker shows maximum possible average handling time (AHT) while the lowest point of the bottom whisker indicates the minimum possible value. Also, the length of the whisker is used to identify if the data skewed.

The asterisk (*) mark at the bottom of the graph indicates the outlier.

Run Chart

Run chart is used to validate if there are any non-randomness in the data. Run chart analysis can tell if the data has trends, oscillation, mixtures or clustering. This non-randomness of the data can be attributed to special causes. The process is stable if it has only common cause or process variation.

Below figure shows the run chart analysis using a statistics software. All data points are plotted in time sequence, and a horizontal reference line is drawn at the median. The data is random if all p-values are greater than 0.05.

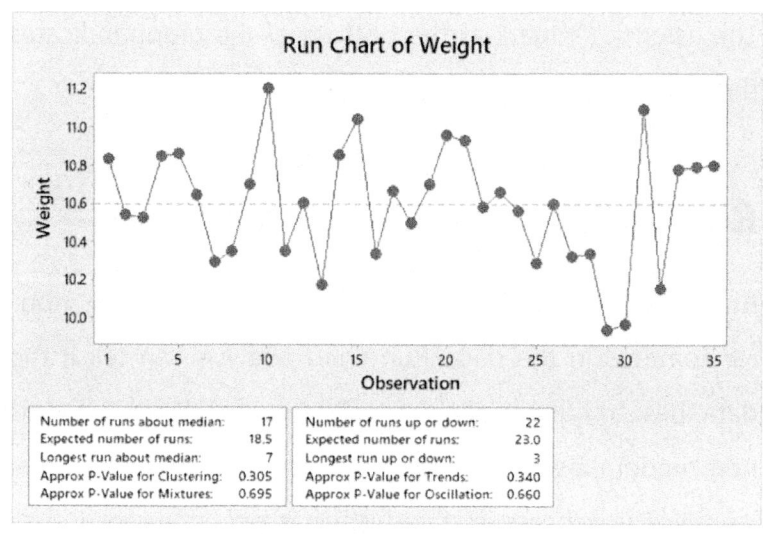

Figure 22: Run Chart

Probability Distribution

The data distribution is the representation of all possible values along with the frequency of occurrence. There are three main types of probability distributions used in Six Sigma; Normal, Binomial and Poisson.

Normal distribution

In statistics, there are various data distributions defined, Normal distribution also known as a bell-shaped curve is the most popular. It is applicable for continuous data.

Characteristics of Normal distribution:

- Data can be summarized using mean and standard deviation.
- It is symmetrical in nature i.e. mean divides data in two equal parts.
- Mean, median and mode are same for a normally distributed data.
- Skewness and Kurtosis is zero (approximately)
- The frequency of data points decreases as we move away from the central line in both the direction hence giving it a bell-like shape.

- 68.27% of data is within +/- 1 standard deviation of the mean, 95.46% is within +/- 2 standard deviation, and 99.73% are within +/- 3 standard deviations.

Binomial distribution

Binomial distribution is suitable for count data. For example, the number of products that have cleared the quality test.

Pre-checks for Binomial Distribution:

- Fixed number of trials
- Each trial is independent (result of one trial should not dictate another trail)
- Each trial has one of the two outcomes: event or non-event
- The probability of the occurrence of event is same for each trail

Binomial distribution can be approximated by a normal distribution if the sample size (n) is large and the probability of defective items is 0.5.

The binomial distribution is relevant when we are calculating defectives.

Defects are any nonconformance of output with the specified requirements. Defective is the unit which is unacceptable for use. A defective item can have multiple defects. Defects, depending on the severity, lead to a defective product. The high severity defects are fatal errors, while the low severity defects are known as non-fatal errors. For example, abusing client on a customer care call is a fatal error but forgetting to greet him is a non-fatal error.

Poisson distribution

Poisson distribution is also suitable for discrete data but applicable for the number of defects, not defectives.

It was developed by French mathematician Simeon Denis Poisson hence the name. The distribution is defined by λ (lambda) which represents both mean and standard deviation. As the λ value increases, Poisson distribution approximates to the normal distribution.

Pre-checks for Poisson distribution:

- Data is the count of events
- All events are independent.
- Average rate does not change over the period of interest.

Two Poisson distribution can be compared using rate of occurrence i.e. λ divided by the observation space.

For example, employee A made 10 errors in 10 calls while employee B made 3 errors in 9 calls.

$$The\ rate\ of\ occurance\ for\ employee\ A = \frac{10}{10} = 1$$

$$The\ rate\ of\ occurance\ for\ employee\ A = \frac{3}{9} = 0.33$$

Hence B is obviously performing better than employee A.

Part 4: Analyze

Process Mapping – VA NVA Analysis

VA NVA Analysis is conducted on the value stream map or a detailed process map.

- VA stands for Value-added activity which means an activity that is creating value for the client
- NVA (Non-value added activity) are the activities that are not adding any value for the customer, for example, waiting time.

Another classification is the ENVA i.e. Essential non-value added activities. These are the activities that are not adding any value to the process, but they help to complete the value-added activities in a better and faster way. For example, a quality audit helps to avoid defects but doesn't add direct value to the process/product.

In Lean methodology, anything that is not 'Value' to the customer is considered as 'Waste' or 'Muda.' 'Muda' is a Japanese term for 'Waste.'

There are eight types of Waste defined which are universally applicable and not just in the manufacturing sector. 'TIMWOODS' is the acronym used to remember all types of waste.

T - Transport

I - Inventory

M - Motion

W - Waiting

O - Over-production

O - Over-processing

D - Defects

S – Skills unutilized

Traditionally there were seven different types of waste defined, but as we progressed further ', Skills unutilized' was also added to the list.

1. **Transport:**

    Unnecessary movements of product and material results in the waste of energy and time, hence adding to cost. Multiple reasons can cause excess transportation, most commonly because of poor layout design or poor process design or over production.

    Examples: Movement of finished goods from one plant to another plant for storage, multiple handoffs

2. **Inventory:**

Excess inventory of finished goods or work-in-progress (WIP) items. Ideally, supply should be equal to demand to avoid finished goods inventory. However, that may not always possible, WIP inventory gets accumulated when production rate of one unit is more than the next.

Examples: Transactions getting accumulated in Quality Auditor's queue as multiple resources are processing transactions simultaneously and pushing completed transactions for audit. Finished goods are waiting in the store room for getting sold in the market as supply is more than demand.

3. **Motion:**

   Unnecessary movement of people. This waste is confused with transportation waste. Transportation is the unnecessary movement of product or material while motion is the unnecessary movement of people. Examples: Trying to find a file, movement to/from the printer.

4. **Waiting:**

   Time wasted in waiting for next process step by man/material. Waiting is the most common form of waste.

Examples: Waiting because of system downtime/machine broke down, an employee waiting to process the transaction as approval is pending.

5. **Over-production:**

   Excess production more than demand or before there is demand. A common cause of over-production is inaccurate or no demand forecasting.

   Examples: Unrequired reports produced, unrequired information shared with the client, training material printed in advance

6. **Over-processing:**

   Processing more than what is required to generate the value expected by the customer. In simple words, adding multiple steps to achieve a goal which can be accomplished using a simple approach.

   Examples: Multiple approvals required for a request, multiple follow-ups.

7. **Defects:**

   Deviation from client shared specifications. A defect can either be fatal or non-fatal. The fatal error results in a defective product which is not accepted by the customer. However, both types of defects should be avoided as either require rework which is a waste of time and money

Example: Incorrect data entry, incorrect price updated online, incorrect invoice generated

8. **Skills un-utilized:**

    Employees' full potential not utilized, this happens when there is a mismatch in the skill set of employee and one required for the job. Attrition is the most common result of this waste.

    Example: Person put on the wrong job

After conducting VA-NVA analysis, the team has the list of causes that are leading to the variation in the process. For example, excess waiting time at 'updating order details in system' step, leading to increasing cycle time.

Failure Mode Effect Analysis (FMEA)

Failure mode effect analysis (FMEA) is the risk management tool that provides a structured approach to discover potential failures that may exist in a process. In six sigma methodology, the FMEA is conducted on the "Future State" to ensure a robust system is developed.

The FMEA consist of following sections:

1. **Process step**: Process map precedes the FMEA, once the map created, list down each block of the process map on an excel file in one column

2. **Potential failure mode**: The next column will be potential failure mode means 'what can go wrong with the process step?'

    For example, 'enter the loan amounts in the application' is a process step, the potential failure mode is that the resource entered wrong details.

3. **Potential failure effect**: For each failure mode, list down the impact.

    For example, if resource entered the wrong amount on the loan application, either it gets approved or rejected which leads to delay in loan disbursement as the team will have to rework on the application.

4. **Severity**: How severe is the potential failure effect?

    The team should rate severity on the scale of 1-10, 1 being the lowest and 10 being the highest. Most of the companies prefer to define the rating guidelines internally. For example, in the service industry, government law violation without warning can be considered the most severe effect.

5. **Potential causes of failure**: Identify the causes that may lead to the failure mode

    For example, the loan amount is updated incorrectly because the resource is new, the numbers are not separated by a comma when updated in the system leading to confusion, etc.

6. **Occurrence**: How often these probable causes of failure can occur?

    The occurrence should be rated on the scale of 1 to 10, 1 being lowest. Companies should define rating scales internally as per historical data. For example, 1 in 1000 can be the highest priority for one company and can be medium or low for another.

7. **Current controls**: What are the control measure in place to avoid failure mode?

    Process controls can be of two types: Prevention and Detection. In prevention control, the system gives warning before the error occurs, and detection controls give warning once the error occurred to avoid it passing to the next stage.

8. **Detection**: How effective is the control measures? Control measures should be rated on the scale of 1-10 where 1 being almost certain that it will detect the error and 10 being absolutely uncertain.
9. **RPN**: Risk Priority Number (RPN) helps in prioritizing all identified risks.

$$RPN = Severity * Occurance * Detection$$

10. **Action items**: The team can decide on a threshold RPN. All RPNs greater than threshold RPN should have an action item to mitigate risk. The objective is that once action items are implemented, the RPN should reduce. There is nothing team can do about 'Severity.' It is a factual number if any failure effect is of highest severity, so it will remain the same irrespective of it occurs or not unless company's priority changes. Hence, you should take 'Detection' and 'Occurrence' in consideration while brainstorming the action items.

Cause Effect diagram

Fish Bone Diagram or Cause-Effect Diagram also known as Ishikawa diagram as first introduced by Kaoru Ishikawa in 1968. Cause Effect Diagram is used to identify the multiple causes leading to an effect.

1. Write down the problem statement (as defined in Define Phase)
2. Draw branches from the problem statement as shown below indicating categories of causes. Mostly used categories are Man, Machine, Material, Method (Process), Mother Nature (Environment, e.g., Market conditions)

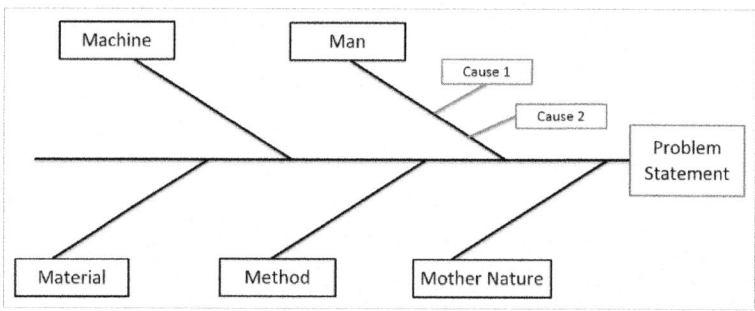

<u>Figure 23: Fishbone Analysis</u>

3. Brainstorm with the focused group to identify the possible causes in each of the criteria.
4. Analyze the causes

Gemba Walk

'Gemba' is a Japanese word which means 'the real place.' In lean six sigma context, 'the real place' means where the work is happening The Gemba walk is:

1. Going to the place where value is created
2. Observe the process
3. Ask relevant questions
4. Learn (identify improvement opportunities)

Gemba walk is a regular activity conducted at a predefined interval. Executives can take Gemba walk once in a week for about 45 to 60 minutes on their own. And at least 2 Gemba walk per quarter with a lean expert. The important point to remember is executive should not treat gemba walk as inspection, else team may try to cover up the real issues.

Correlation

Correlation analysis is used when both X and Y are continuous data and to determine the association between them.

The correlation between two parameters is indicated using correlation coefficient also known as Pearson's correlation coefficient, indicated as 'r'. The value of 'r' can vary from -1 to +1.

'-1' indicate negative correlation which means an increase in the value of X lead to decrease in 'Y' while '+1' shows positive correlation which means both parameters will move in one direction.

The no correlation between X and Y is indicated by zero value of 'r'. As a thumb rule, <-0.85 and >+0.85 is considered to be a strong correlation.

Statistical software can be used to conduct correlation analysis. The result will have 'r' and p-value for the analysis.

P-value > 0.05 means there is no correlation between Y and X.

Correlation is a useful and simple tool used to determine the relationship between two parameters. However, correlation can only give linear relation. Also, it fails to tell the degree of association i.e. if X is changed by one unit what is the impact on Y. Will it also change by 1 unit assuming they have positive correlation or more than one unit?

Regression

Regression is also applicable when both X and Y are continuous. Unlike correlation, regression conduct association test and gives the degree of association.

A typical regression equation is $Y = f(X)$

Simple Linear Regression

Use simple linear regression when there is one X and one Y. A linear relation is a trend in data that can be represented using a straight line.

The simple linear regression equation is $Y = mX + C + E$

m: is the slope of the straight line

C: is the intercept.

E: is the error

X: Input independent variable also called as predictor

Y: Output dependent variable also called as response

Below shows the statistical software output of the regression analysis.

```
Regression Analysis: y versus x

The regression equation is
y = - 0.4618 + 1.014 x


S = 3.03740   R-Sq = 98.9%   R-Sq(adj) = 98.9%


Analysis of Variance

Source       DF       SS       MS         F       P
Regression    1   249951   249951   27092.62   0.000
Error       298     2749        9
Total       299   252700
```

Figure 24: Simple Linear Equation Results

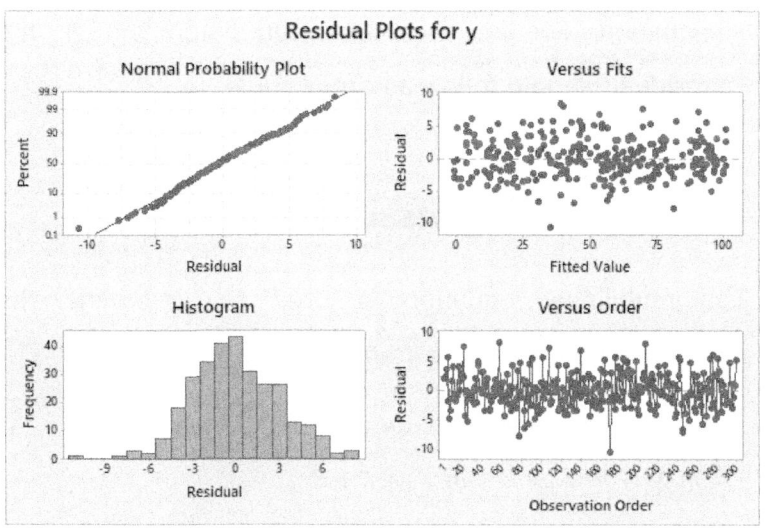

Figure 25: Simple Linear Regression Residual Graph

Data Interpretation:

- P-value<0.05 = Significant correlation between X & Y.
- The R-Sq is the coefficient of determination. If R-Sq is 75%, this means 75% of the linear variation in 'Y' is explained by 'X.' The R-Sq greater than or equal to 75% is considered to be a good model.
- If P<0.05 while R-Sq is not high enough, then other variables (Xs) should also be considered or non-linear regression should be used.
- Residual is the difference between the original value of Y and the value of Y calculated using regression equation. For an acceptable regression model, the residuals should follow a normal curve.

Multilinear regression

The multilinear equation is used to determine the relationship between one Y and multiple Xs.

The multilinear regression equation is
$Y = m_1 X_1 + m_2 X_2 + \ldots + m_n X_n + C + E$

Below shows the statistical software output of the multilinear regression analysis

Regression Analysis: Biomass versus Depth, Area1, Cover, Area2

```
Analysis of Variance

Source       DF    Adj SS   Adj MS  F-Value  P-Value
Regression    4   1330434   332609    32.16    0.001
  Depth       1     99255    99255     9.60    0.027
  Area1       1     22345    22345     2.16    0.202
  Cover       1      3187     3187     0.31    0.603
  Area2       1    699054   699054    67.60    0.000
Error         5     51706    10341
Total         9   1382141


Model Summary

      S    R-sq  R-sq(adj)  R-sq(pred)
101.692  96.26%     93.27%      65.11%


Coefficients

Term         Coef   SE Coef  T-Value  P-Value   VIF
Constant       86       125     0.68    0.524
Depth      -15.93      5.14    -3.10    0.027  4.11
Area1        2.42      1.65     1.47    0.202  1.36
Cover        1.83      3.29     0.56    0.603  1.18
Area2       3.074     0.374     8.22    0.000  3.71


Regression Equation

Biomass = 86 - 15.93 Depth + 2.42 Area1 + 1.83 Cover + 3.074 Area2


Fits and Diagnostics for Unusual Observations

Obs  Biomass    Fit   Resid  Std Resid
  3    755.0  844.3   -89.3      -2.14  R

R  Large residual
```

Figure 26: Multilinear Regression Analysis Session Window Result

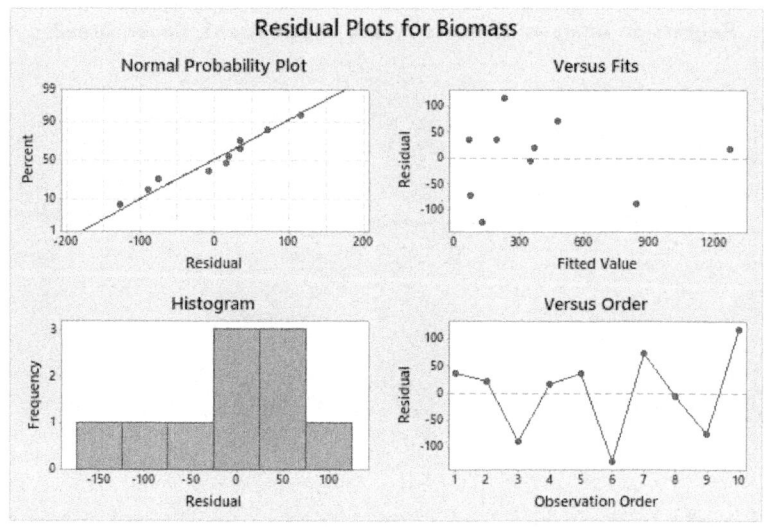

Figure 27: Multilinear Regression Analysis Residual Plot

Data interpretation

- P-value<0.05 = Significant correlation between X & Y.
- VIF, Variance inflation factor is used to identify if there is a correlation among the Xs. VIF>5 means Xs are correlated with each other. Hence this regression model is not valid
- R-Sq > 75% = accepted regression model as 75% of the linear variation in 'Y' is explained by considered 'Xs.'
- Residual should follow a normal curve.

Hypothesis Testing

Hypothesis testing is used to statistically validate a theory defined for a sample or among multiple samples.

The first step is to establish a null hypothesis and an alternate hypothesis.

- Null Hypothesis (H_0) is general 'no effect' hypothesis.
- Alternate Hypothesis (H_1) is the condition that researcher is trying to prove right.

Hypothesis testing helps the researcher to find sufficient statistical evidence to say that alternative theory is correct until then assume null hypothesis is true.

For a six sigma project, hypothesis testing is used to validate the set target, improvements achieved, and prioritize root causes.

For example, the average handling time for a process is 153 mins as per last quarter data, and senior management wants to improve it to 130 mins average, to check if this is a valid target, use hypothesis testing.

$H_0: \mu_T = Y$

$H_1: \mu_T < Y$

μ_T: The target population mean (130 mins)

Y: The sample mean i.e. calculated mean as per last quarter data i.e. 153 mins.

Type I & Type II Error

A statistical test can never be 100% certain; the result can only be accurate with some level of confidence.

In hypothesis testing, there are two possible errors

1. **Type I error**: Rejecting null hypothesis when it is true.

    If a researcher is making type I error, s/he is acting assuming there is an effect. Hence this error also referred as **Producer's risk**.

    The chances of making Type I error is denoted using α (alpha) symbol, which is the level of significance set for the hypothesis testing. If α is 0.05, this means researcher is willing to accept 5% chances that s/he is wrong in rejecting the null hypothesis.

    The statistical software generates a probability denoted as 'p-value' which refers the likelihood of rejecting the null hypothesis when it is correct. Hence if the p-value is less than α, we can reject the null hypothesis and can conclude that there is enough evidence to prove that alternate theory is correct.

2. **Type II error**: Failing to reject the null hypothesis when it is false.

   Type II error is **Consumer's risk** because even though there was an effect, the producer did not act on it hence the consumer did not get the better results.

   The probability of making type II error is referred as β (Beta). The power of the test is in giving the correct result, i.e., accepting alternate hypothesis when null is false because that was the whole objective of conducting a hypothesis test. Hence the power of the test is referred using $(1-\beta)$.

		NULL HYPOTHESIS	
		ACCEPT	REJECT
NULL HYPOTHESIS	TRUE	$(1-\alpha)$	Type I error (α), Significance Level, Producer's Risk
	FALSE	Type II error (β) Consumer's Risk	$(1-\beta)$, Power of the test

Figure 28: Type I and II Error

Hypothesis Test Roadmap

There are multiple hypothesis tests available and should be utilized as per data type and the objective.

Below shows the flow charts that can be used to select right hypothesis testing:

1. **Continuous Normal Data (Parametric Test)**

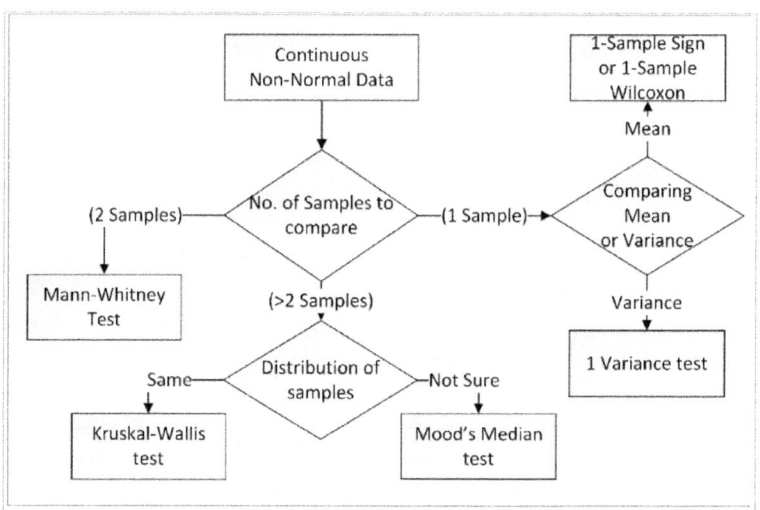

Figure 29: Roadmap for Continuous Normal data

2. Continuous Non-Normal Data (Non-Parametric Test)

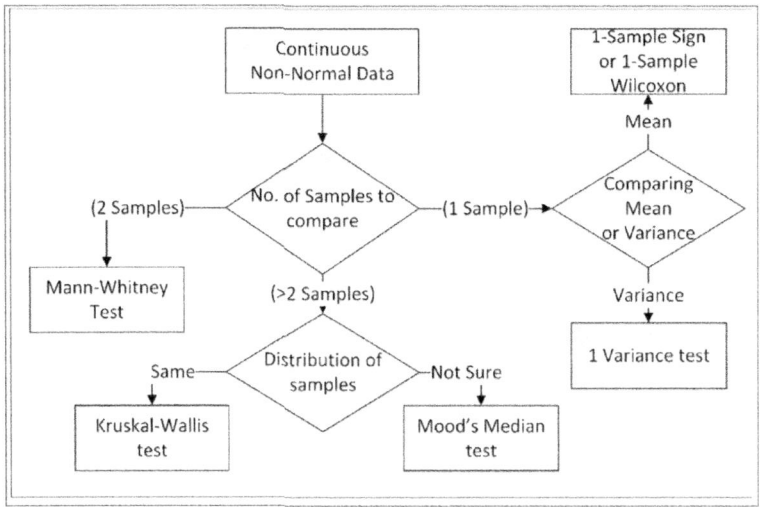

Figure 30: Roadmap for Continuous Non-normal data

3. Discrete Data – Binomial

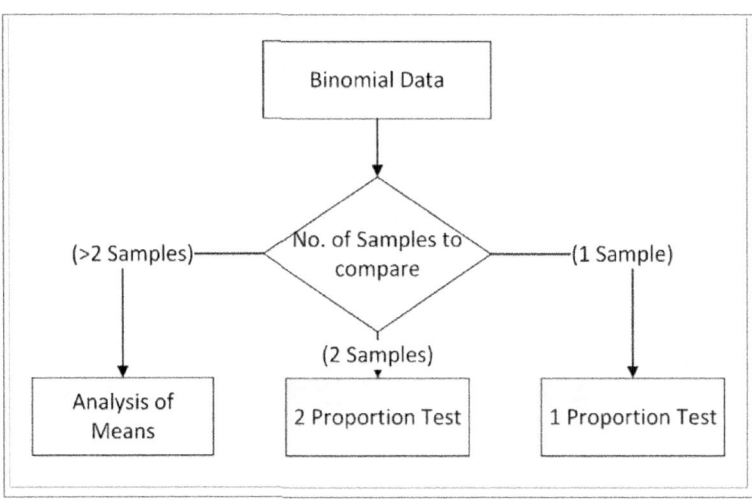

Figure 31: Roadmap for Binomial Data

Parametric Hypothesis Test (continuous normal data)

T-TEST

The t-test is used when the data is continuous and normally distributed.

There are three different types of t-test can be utilized depending on how many samples are in consideration:

One sample t-test

One sample t-test is used to compare population mean with a defined value using sample data.

The test uses sample standard deviation to calculate population standard deviation. If there is a large difference between the sample mean and the specified test mean (given value), then the test concludes that it is highly unlikely that population means will be anywhere near test mean.

Assumptions

1. Sample data follows normal distribution
2. Sample data is random

Consider sample data of the average handling time of a process with mean 4.51 minutes and standard deviation of 0.2878.

To validate if the goal of reducing population mean to 4 minutes is significant, use 1-sample t-test.

H_0: Hypothesized Mean (4 min) = Population Mean (μ)

H_1: Hypothesized Mean > Population Mean (μ)

The following illustration shows the typical result of the t-test:

```
One-Sample T: Average Handling time
Test of µ = 4 vs > 4

Variable              N    Mean   StDev  SE Mean   95% Lower Bound      T      P
Average Handling time 49  4.5095  0.2878  0.0411            4.4405  12.39  0.000
```

Figure 32: One Sample t-test results

As P is 0.000 i.e. less than significant level of 0.05, hence reject null hypothesis which means set target is significant

Two sample t-test

Two sample t-test is used to compare population mean of the two sample data.

Assumption:
1. Sample data follows normal distribution

2. Sample data is random
3. Samples are independent to each other

H_0: (Population mean (μ_1) - Population mean (μ_2)) = 0

H_1: ($\mu_1 - \mu_2$) ≠ 0 or $\mu_1 > \mu_2$ or $\mu_1 < \mu_2$

To check if there is an improvement in average handling time post implementing six sigma project as compared to the pre-data, hypothesis testing can be used. If both data sets are normal, we can use two sample t-test.

H_0: Pre-improvement mean (μ_1) - Post-improvement mean (μ_2) = 0

H_1: Pre-improvement mean (μ_1) - Post-improvement mean (μ_2) > 0

Below shows two sample t-test result,

```
Two-Sample T-Test and CI: Pre-Improvement, Post Improvement

Two-sample T for Pre-Improvement vs Post Improvement

                  N    Mean   StDev  SE Mean
Pre-Improvement   49  4.509   0.288    0.041
Post Improvement  49  4.250   0.254    0.036

Difference = μ (Pre-Improvement) - μ (Post Improvement)
Estimate for difference:  0.2595
95% lower bound for difference:  0.1684
T-Test of difference = 0 (vs >): T-Value = 4.73  P-Value = 0.000  DF = 94
```

Figure 33: Two Sample t-test

Data Interpretation:

- The P-value is less than significant level of 5%. Hence we can reject the null hypothesis, and hence conclude pre-improvement mean is greater than the post improvement mean.

Paired t-test

Paired t-test is used to compare two population mean for the paired observations. For example, the cycle time of an employee before refresher training as compared to after training. The data should be collected for the same object with only one variable changing (training in this scenario).

Assumptions:

1. Sample data is continuous and follows normal distribution
2. Observations must be paired
3. The difference should be normally distributed.

$H_0: \mu_1 - \mu_2 = 0$

$H_1: \mu_1 - \mu_2 > 0$

Below shows the typical output of statistical software.

```
Paired T-Test and CI: Before Refresher Training, After Refresher Training

Paired T for Before Refresher Training - After Refresher Training

                          N     Mean    StDev   SE Mean
Before Refresher Trainin  35   4.5472   0.2437   0.0412
After Refresher Training  35   4.9736   0.3087   0.0522
Difference                35  -0.4264   0.3674   0.0621


95% CI for mean difference: (-0.5526, -0.3002)
T-Test of mean difference = 0 (vs ≠ 0): T-Value = -6.87  P-Value = 0.000
```

Figure 34: Paired t-test

Data Interpretation:

- The P-value is less than significant level of 5%. Hence we can reject the null hypothesis, and conclude there is a change in performance post refresher training.

ANOVA Test

ANOVA test is used to compare the mean of two or more populations. ANOVA is used when Y is continuous, and X's are discrete. For example, to check if employee shift timing (APAC, EMEA, AMER) impacts case resolution, ANOVA can be used. Here the number of cases resolved is Y which is a continuous data and shifts is X which is a discrete data.

Null Hypothesis = H_0: All variances are equal

Alternate Hypothesis = H_1: Not all variances are equal

Similar to another hypothesis tests, if the p-value is less than alpha, then you can conclude that at least one of the mean is different.

There are three types of ANOVA:

1. One-Way ANOVA: To determine if the means of two or more groups differ
2. Balance ANOVA: To determine if the means of two or more groups differ when you have multiple factors, but requires a balanced design
3. General linear model: To determine if the means of two or more groups differ when you include random factors, covariates, or a mix of crossed

and nested factors, perform a general linear model analysis

One-Way ANOVA

One-way ANOVA is used to compare the means of responses for multiple groups at different levels.

For example, in a call center, you want to test if pre-hiring English test grade has any impact on the average handling time of the employee. Here, average handling time is the continuous response, and the test score range can be the different levels (factors).

Figure 35 shows the statistical software output of ANOVA test, where we are trying to compare hardness of blend of paint.

```
One-way ANOVA: Blend 1, Blend 2, Blend 3, Blend 4

Method

Null hypothesis         All means are equal
Alternative hypothesis  At least one mean is different
Significance level      α = 0.05

Equal variances were assumed for the analysis.


Factor Information

Factor  Levels  Values
Factor       4  Blend 1, Blend 2, Blend 3, Blend 4


Analysis of Variance

Source  DF  Adj SS  Adj MS  F-Value  P-Value
Factor   3   281.7   93.90     6.02    0.004
Error   20   312.1   15.60
Total   23   593.8


Model Summary

      S   R-sq  R-sq(adj)  R-sq(pred)
3.95012  47.44%    39.56%      24.32%


Means

Factor   N   Mean  StDev       95% CI
Blend 1  6  14.73   3.36  (11.37, 18.10)
Blend 2  6   8.57   5.50  ( 5.20, 11.93)
Blend 3  6  12.98   3.73  ( 9.62, 16.35)
Blend 4  6  18.07   2.64  (14.70, 21.43)

Pooled StDev = 3.95012
```

Figure 35: One Way ANOVA result

Data Interpretation

- As P-value in 'Analysis of Variance' is less than 0.05 (alpha), you can reject the null hypothesis,

concluding there is a significant difference in the mean of the population group.
- R^2 in 'Model Summary' represents how well the variation in data can be explained using this model.
- R^2 (pred) means how well the model can predict the responses for new observations.
- The model is considered good that minimize S and maximize the three R^2 values

Two-Way ANOVA (Balanced ANOVA)

Two-way ANOVA is used to prioritize potential discrete Xs. Unlike one-way ANOVA more than one Xs can be considered in Two-way ANOVA.

Similar to another hypothesis testing, P-value < 0.05 (alpha), indicates that you can reject null hypothesis, concluding there is significant difference in the mean of the population group i.e. respective X is significant

General Linear Model (GLM)

General linear model is similar to two-way ANOVA test used to prioritize potential discrete Xs (two or more than two). The only difference is that two-way ANOVA test requires a balanced design while GLM can be used for non-balanced design as well.

A balanced design has an equal number of observations for all possible combinations of factor levels while an unbalanced design has an unequal number of observations.

Non-Parametric Test (Continuous Non-normal data)

Similar to parametric test, non-parametric tests are also used for continuous data but when the data distribution is unknown or not normal.

Since the distribution is unknown, the median is compared instead of the mean. The non-parametric test requires the data to be an independent sample. These tests are not as robust as their parametric counterpart hence you have to be careful while rejecting the null hypothesis.

The statistical software result of the non-parametric test also generates p-value, which is if less than significance level of 0.05, reject the null hypothesis.

1-Sample Sign Test

1-sample sign test is non-parametric equivalent to 1-sample t-test, used to compare population median with the target.

H_0: η (population median) = η_0 (hypothesized median / target)

H_1: $\eta \neq \eta_0$ OR $\eta > \eta_0$ OR $\eta < \eta_0$

1-Sample Wilcoxon Test

1-sample Wilcoxon test is another non-parametric equivalent to 1-sample t-test, used to compare population median with the target.

However, unlike 1-sample sign test, it assumes that the data follows symmetrical distribution like the uniform or cauchy distributions. If this assumption is not validated, it is safe to use 1-sample sign test.

H_0: η (population median) = $η_0$ (hypothesized median / target)

H_1: η ≠ $η_0$ OR η > $η_0$ OR η < $η_0$

Mann-Whitney Test

Mann-Whitney test is similar to 2-Sample test used to compare two sample data. The result indicates if population median of two sample data differs also gives the range that includes the difference between two populations median.

Assumption: Both sample data follows similarly shaped distribution. For example, both non-normal and right skewed.

H_0: $η_1$ (population1 median) = $η_2$ (population2 median)

H_1: $η_1$ ≠ $η_2$ OR $η_1$ > $η_2$ OR $η_1$ < $η_2$

Kruskal-Wallis Test

Kruskal-Wallis test is non-parametric test equivalent to the one-way ANOVA test, used to compare population median of two or more groups.

Assumption: All groups follow a similarly shaped distribution. For example, all non-normal and right skewed.

H_0: All population medians are equal

H_1: At least one of the population median is not equal

Mood's Median Test

Mood's median test is another non-parametric test equivalent to the one-way ANOVA test, used to compare population median of two or more groups. However, unlike Kruskal-Wallis test, it does not assume that all groups follow similarly shared distribution.

Hence when you are not sure of data distribution, it is safe to use Mood's median test.

H_0: All population medians are equal

H_1: At least one of the population median is not equal

Binomial Hypothesis Test

Proportion test

1-Proportion Test

The 1 proportion test used to compare the proportion of a population with the target or reference value. This test can be used to compare the number of defectives. The statistical software output gives a range that is likely to include the population proportion.

H_0: p (population proportion) = p_0 (hypothesized proportion / target)

H_1: $p \neq p_0$ OR $p > p_0$ OR $p < p_0$

2-Proportion Test

The 2 proportion test used to compare the proportion of two populations.

H_0: p_1 (population proportion) = p_2 (hypothesized proportion / target)

H_1: $p_1 \neq p_2$ OR $p_1 > p_2$ OR $p_1 < p_2$

Analysis of Means (ANOM)

ANOM is similar to ANOVA, used to compare means of two or more population. One major difference between is that ANOVA assumes the data distribution is normal while ANOM can be used for normal, binomial or poisson distribution.

Similar to ANOVA, P-value < 0.05 (alpha), indicates that you can reject null hypothesis, concluding there is significant difference in the mean of the population group i.e. respective X is significant

Part 5: Improve

Idea Generation

Benchmarking

Benchmarking is the process of evaluating current performance of an organization or a department against best practices. Benchmarking can be done internally or externally.

1. Internal Benchmarking: Team will look into systems of another department with in same organization and will try to apply concepts to their department.
2. External Benchmarking: Team will look into systems of another company to identify improvement opportunities. It can be done within the same industry or different industries.

The typical brainstorming process is:

1. Create process map
2. Identify area of opportunities
3. Understand how other's process applies to our problem areas
4. Prepare a plan to implement best practices.

The first two steps i.e. creating process map and identifying an area of opportunity is already completed till 'Analyze' phase. At this stage, the team should try to identify best practices internally or externally that can be used for the root causes identified.

Brainstorming

Brainstorming is a team activity where the team tries to come up with multiple options. Brainstorming is applicable at every stage of lean six sigma project as it's a team effort. Participants are asked to share their thoughts on the problem, any idea that they think relevant for solving the problem. Do not criticize or reward ideas during brainstorming. The quantity of idea is more important than the quality of ideas. Each idea will either help to create a solution or triggering additional thought process.

There are two types of brainstorming.

1. **Individual brainstorming:** an Individual person can try to brainstorm on their own to develop multiple ideas. Individual brainstorming allows people to think freely without worrying about other's opinion. But they may not be able to develop idea completely because of your limited knowledge and experience.

2. **Group brainstorming:** Group of relevant people discuss a problem and try to come up with the idea. Lateral thinking and various viewpoints help to develop idea completely. But in group brainstorming, an individual may worry about other's opinion and will not share their idea freely. Also, they may forget the original idea while waiting for their turn to come.

In most of the practical scenarios, there is a moderator in a brainstorming session to guide the discussion. His/her job is to ensure participants are discussing points relevant to the problem and everybody got a chance to participate.

Lean Tools

The team can use various lean tools to improve the process. The Toyota Productions system is already discussed in the part-I of the book. You can use Just-in-time method, Jidoka, Heijunka, Standardize work, Kanban and Kaizen as solutions for the identified problems if relevant. 5S, Visual Andon, and Poka-Yoke can also be used for resolving identified problems.

5S

5S is a lean tool used for organizing the workplace. 5S represents 5 Japanese words all starting with 'S,' Seiri (Sort), Seiton (Set in Order), Seiso (Shine), Seiketsu (Standardize), and Shitsuke (Sustain). It was invented in Japan to enable Just in time production. Unlike general norms, 5S has application in manufacturing as well as service industries

1. Seiri mean Sort i.e. segregating what is needed and not needed. This is the most challenging and important step of implementing 5S as the human tendency is to preserve everything.

For example, Computer Desktop has so many files that may or may not be always required, which makes it difficult to find the desired file. Similar is the case with team shared drives.

2. Seiton means Set in order i.e. defining a place for everything and keep it in its designated location.

   For example in shared drives, the nomenclature for folders should be such that anyone can understand where to save a particular file.

3. Seiso means Shine i.e. keeping everything clean. Cleaning frequency should be defined to ensure everything is cleaned regularly.

   For example, shared drive should clean on a regular interval to ensure non-relevant files are archived.

4. Seiketsu mean Standardize i.e. the instruction to maintain and monitor first three steps should be clearly defined. 5S is not a one-time job; it is a regular activity. Hence once the required frequency to repeat first three steps is agreed, it should be standardized. Also, it helps in sharing best practices rather than re-inventing the wheel.

5. Shitsuke mean Sustain. It is all about building self-discipline. All these steps should be done without

being told to do. The process should be set to regularly audit and monitor for all the departments.

Visual Andon

'Andon' means 'Signal.' Visual Andon refers to a visual signal that shows the status of the process. It helps in raising alert whenever there is action required. Visual Andon is mostly used with Jidoka to aid operator who is managing more than one automated machine. In the service sector, the supervisor takes help of Visual Andon to see if all processes are working as per plan. Andon is colored coded to indicate status:

1. Green: Process is running as planned/expected
2. Yellow/Amber: Process/Machine is down as per planned maintenance, needs some monitoring
3. Red: Process/Machine is down because of unexpected reason, and immediate action is required

Poka-Yoke

Poka-Yoke is Japan term which means 'mistake-proofing.' Poka-Yoke prevents in converting errors into defects or defective products hence improving quality. There are two types of mistake proofing done:

1. Preventive Poka-Yoke: Mistake proofing to avoid the occurrence of error. Preventive Poka-Yoke is also called as Control or Shutdown Poka Yoke. For example, Account is blocked if incorrect password updated for multiple time. MS Excel gives warming to save the document while closing if not saved already. Computer plugs are designed such that they can be plugged in a particular way hence avoiding system damage. Color coding is done on wires and socket so that they are plugged in respective socket only.
2. Detection Poka-Yoke: Mistake proofing to alert as and when an error occurs. This is also called as Warning or Attention Poke Yoke. For example, Car to give warming for over speeding or for not wearing seat belts, Smoke Detector, Notifications generated for the orders/transactions which may miss SLAs

Selection and Prioritization of Solution

Pugh Matrix

Pugh matrix is a tool to compare multiple alternatives against the baseline. For any situation, as-is performance will be the baseline practice; the team can come up with multiple solutions to evaluate against the baseline.

Follow these simple steps to create a Pugh matrix:

1. Identify criteria to evaluate the solutions which are critical for business. Let's say C1, C2, C3, and C4.
2. Give weightage to all the ideas. Since we are comparing the as-is situation, the baseline will be scored as zero.

Criteria	Weight	Baseline	Idea 1	Idea 2	Idea 3
C1	2	0			
C2	3	0			
C3	4	0			
C4	1	0			

3. Rank each idea against each criteria. For example, if idea 1 is better than baseline on C1, it gets '+1' score.if it's performance is same as baseline give it '0' and if it gets worse than baseline give it '-1'.

Criteria	Weight	Baseline	Idea 1	Idea 2	Idea 3
C1	2	0	-1	0	+1
C2	3	0	0	-1	+1
C3	4	0	+1	+1	+1
C4	1	0	0	0	-1

4. Now multiply weight with the idea score

Criteria	Weight	Baseline	Idea 1	Idea 2	Idea 3
C1	2	0	-2	0	+2
C2	3	0	0	-3	+3
C3	4	0	+4	+4	+4
C4	1	0	0	0	-1

5. Sum all scores to get the total score for each idea. The idea that got maximum score will get the priority

Criteria	Weight	Baseline	Idea 1	Idea 2	Idea 3
C1	2	0	-2	0	+2
C2	3	0	0	-3	+3
C3	4	0	+4	+4	+4
C4	1	0	0	0	-1
Total Score			+2	+1	+8

Multi-voting

Multi-voting is another technique used to prioritize ideas. The group of individuals who have knowledge and experience of the process in the discussion is asked to brainstorm and generate the list of ideas to improve identified X's.

Each focus group member is given N/3 votes where N is the number of ideas generated. Tally the votes, remove ideas with a fewer number of votes. Repeat the process if required, stop when the team has selected top 4-5 X's.

Introduction to Design of Experiment

The design of Experiments is a statistical tool to understand the operating range of the critical Xs finalized in the Analyze phase.

$Y = f(X)$

Since Y is a dependent variable which is a function of Xs, hence to ensure Y is within specification limit given by the client, the operating range of X should be defined and maintained. The regression equation described in the previous section cannot be used here as it may not include all the variables. Moreover, the application of regression in Analyze phase is to validate if X is a critical factor.

The design of experiments helps in validating all the Xs together to identify the optimized value of X to get desired value of X.

Let's assume the process has only one factor impacting Y. Here regression model can be used.

$Y = 10 + 3X$

The specification limits for Y are 40 to 70.

$$If\ Y = 40\ then\ X = \frac{40 - 10}{3} = 10$$

$$If\ Y = 70\ then\ X = \frac{70 - 10}{3} = 20$$

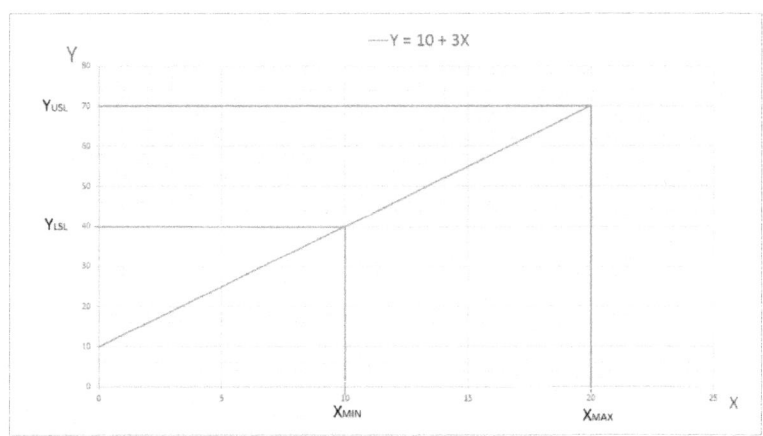

Figure 36 Design of Experiment

To maintain Y within specification limit, X should be greater than 10 and less than 20.

However, the system will have measurement error, for example, the standard deviation of the measurement system is equal to $\sigma_M=3$ as per GRR.

Adjusting the value of Y to avoid measurement error:

$$Y_{USL\ Adjusted} = Y_{USL} - 3\sigma_M = 70 - 3*3 = 61$$

$$Y_{LSL\ Adjusted} = Y_{LSL} + 3\sigma_M = 40 + 3*3 = 49$$

Hence the X operating limits to maintain adjusted specification limit of Y is 13 to 17.

Considering another example, in a six sigma project, team has found English test and Aptitude test scores are significant factors for average handling time of the resources. The team now wants to find out optimum level of cut off for English test and Aptitude test to minimize average handling time.

X1 = English Test Cutoff = 20 or 25

X2 = Aptitude Test Cutoff = 20 or 25

$Number\ of\ experimental\ run = Number\ of\ Levels^{Number\ of\ factors}$

$= 2^2 = 4$

The runs can be ordered either using Yates order or generating random numbers.

Arranging the runs using Yates order, the sequence will be as follows:

English Test Score	Aptitude Test Score
20	20
20	25
25	20

| 25 | 25 |

Conduct repetitive experiments with the above four combinations of Xs, capture the average handling time to compare which combination is giving highest results.

Validation of Improvement

The team can decide to implement the solution across all sites/products/processes if required or they can conduct pilot and then replicate across other locations depending on the pilot learning. Once the improvement plan is implemented, the team should re-baseline performance to validate improvement.

1. Prepare Data Summary
2. Calculate process capability
    a. Sigma level (compare with the one calculated in measure phase)
    b. Cp, Cpk
3. Conduct hypothesis test: to validate if the improvement has significantly improved compared to earlier baseline

Part 6: Control

Process Control Plan

A control plan is a document prepared to ensure that the performance improvement achieved is maintained and sustained. The control plan allocates responsibility to an individual to take care of any variation in the X's.

The key component of the control plans are:

1. Independent variations (Xs): The Xs identified, validated, finalized and improved as part of six sigma process should be documented in the first column in the control plan
2. Data Type: Continuous or discrete data
3. Unit of Measure: For example, is it an hour, a minute or second for average handling time?
4. Specifications: Upper and lower specification limits set during improvement phase as part of Design of Experiment
5. Data Source: From where the data is collected?
6. Data collection method: How data is collected?
7. Data collection frequency: Data captured every hour, daily, monthly or yearly?
8. Sample Size: All data points (population) obtained or sample consider for statistical analysis?

9. Control Method: How are we monitoring or controlling Xs. For example, poka-yoke implemented, 100% inspection/audit, visual controls are in place, or just control charts used to monitor the Xs
10. Corrective Measure: Corrective plans if special cause variations observed in Xs
11. Owner: The team member who is responsible for monitoring and controlling X
12. Accountable/Escalation Point: The manager/leader who should ensure owner fulfilled responsibility and hold accountability to monitor and control independent variables

Statistical Process Control

Statistical process control is to use control charts to capture the fluctuation in Xs over a period.

Control chart roadmap

Depending on the data type and the method of data collection (individual data points or subgroups), relevant control charts should be selected.

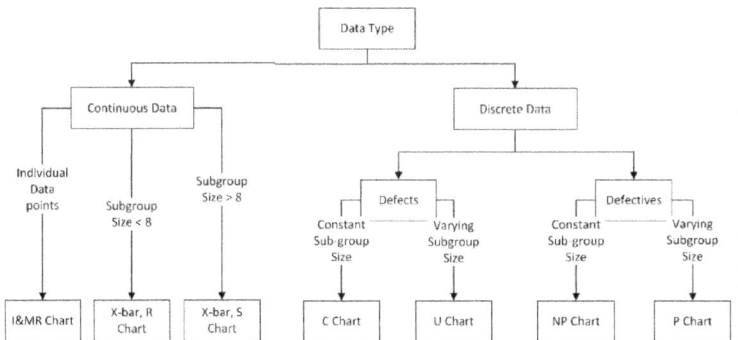

Figure 37: Control Chart Roadmap

Control Limits

Below shows a statistical software output of the control charts.

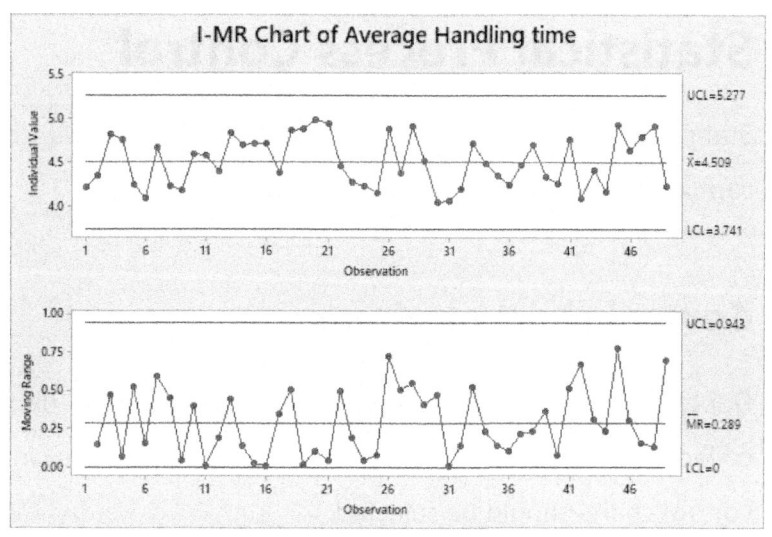

Figure 38: I-MR control chart

The center line in Individual value chart indicates the average performance while the first and the third line represents upper control limit (UCL) and lower control limit (LCL).

$UCL = Process\ mean + 3\ Standard\ Deviation$

$LCL = Process\ mean - 3\ Standard\ Deviation$

UCL and LCL are the control limits of the process, calculated using historical data, hence will change over a period. Data fluctuation within control limit is considered as common cause variation, but if any point is outside of control limits, this mean process has some special causes that should be analyzed. The process where all the data points are within UCL and LCL is a stable process or in-control.

Most of the statistical software conduct the following test to identify special causes:

Test 1: One point more than 3σ from center line - gives the strongest evidence of lack of control

Test 2: Nine points in a row on the same side of the center line

Test 3: Six points in a row, all increasing or all decreasing

Test 4: Fourteen points in a row, alternating up and down

Test 5: Two out of three points more than 2σ from the center line (same side)

Test 6: Four out of five points more than 1σ from center line (same side)

Test 7: Fifteen points in a row within 1σ of the center line (either side) – This helps in identifying if there is stratification in the process.

Test 8: Eight points in a row more than 1σ from center line (either side)

Institutionalize Solution

Institutionalize is the process of creating consistency and uniformity across the organization concerning the process improvement. Institutionalization help in saving time by avoiding re-invention of the wheel.

It's difficult to institutionalize any improvements without an established system and tools. The organization should invest in setting up tools and systems to ensure all improvement projects are closed only after updating details in the central tracker. And whenever team faces any issue, they can go back to improvement central tracker to search possible solutions. This helps in saving time in reworking on a six sigma project.

Project Closure

A six sigma project is considered closed when it's signed off by all relevant stakeholder. In most of the organization, Master Black Belt and Project champion both give final sign-off once details review conducted with the Black belt. The project findings should be documented and stored in the organization's knowledge repository for further reference. Then the project is handed over to the process owner.

The handover document should have:

1. Updated process map and FMEA
2. Control Plan
3. Statistical process control charts
4. Schedule of the review meeting

Printed in Great Britain
by Amazon